your CRYSTALS
your JOURNEY
your JOURNAL

DISCOVER YOUR UNIQUE CRYSTAL CODE

TERESA DELLBRIDGE

GODSFIELD

An Hachette UK company
www.hachette.co.uk

First published in Great Britain in 2022 by Godsfield,
an imprint of Octopus Publishing Group Ltd.
Carmelite House, 50 Victoria Embankment
London, EC4y 0DZ
www.octopusbooks.co.uk

ISBN 978-1-841-81519-0

A CIP catalogue record for this book is available from the British Library

Printed and bound in China

10 9 8 7 6 5 4 3 2 1

Publisher: Lucy Pessell
Designer: Hannah Coughlin
Editor: Sarah Kennedy
Editorial Assistant: Emily Martin
Senior Production Manager: Peter Hunt

Some of this material was previously published in *Your Crystal Code* by Godsfield Press.

This book is not intended as an alternative to personal medical advice. The reader should consult a physician in all matters relating to health and particularly in respect of any symptoms which may require diagnosis or medical attention.

CONTENTS

INTRODUCTION

Enter the world of crystals and be prepared to find true magic in your life. Crystals were formed within the Earth millions of years ago and carry with them the wisdom of the ages.

While all crystals absorb and emit subtle energy, each individual crystal type has a unique vibrational "signature". Each crystal has a symmetrical structure at atomic level, built with geometric precision. While it may appear tranquil and still, at the crystal's molecular level it is a powerhouse of energy. This "energy" is what endows a crystal with its attributes and defines the gifts it brings.

Through the ages crystals have been worn for their beauty, as symbols of power and divinity, or for their therapeutic and beneficial effects. They have been used in magic and to enhance spirituality. Many people believe that crystals are centres or channels of spiritual powers. People who worship Nature see crystals as carrying the special blessing of the Mother Goddess. Others believe that crystals are merely convenient tools for focusing their mental energies. Whatever your perspective, in the following pages you will discover your own special crystals that form a code that will help to enhance your life in a variety of ways. Through a series of rituals, exercises and journaling prompts, you will explore which crystals you feel a connection to, and unlock the ways in which you can use them in your life. Sometimes the crystals will help you with difficulties you've been dealing with for a while; sometimes, they might show you something you didn't even know you needed.

Note: You may find it useful to record yourself reading the visualizations and meditations aloud so that you can listen to them while you perform the rituals, rather than trying to read at the same time.

YOUR CRYSTAL JOURNAL

As you choose, care for and use your crystals, your knowledge and experience are growing. Record your impressions and thoughts in this personal journal, kept especially for you as you journey toward identifying your unique crystal code and gain a deeper understanding of yourself.

This will be a valuable storehouse of knowledge as you become more familiar with crystals. Impressions may come to you through the crystals, or you may feel that you know something about a crystal that is not in this or any other book. You may read or hear information about crystals that is especially interesting, or you may achieve an effect with a crystal that is particularly memorable.

Working with crystals allows you to experience and tap into thoughts, feelings and senses that you may not have explored before. Crystal energy opens your intuition and encourages you to recall past experiences and memories that you may have suppressed or simply forgotten – allowing you to move forward. Taking the time to write about these revelations can help you clarify how they make you feel – and these notes are also a useful tool to look back on as you continue your journey.

Most worthy of note may be dreams that you have or experiences you go through while meditating. But most of all, there is the matter of choosing each of your eight crystals – your Personality, Relaxation, Healing, Protection, Love, Meditation, Money and Success Crystals – and exploring how you feel about each one. All of these things can be recorded in your journal.

Once you have chosen each of your crystals and used them in the exercises, you will have the "code" for balance, harmony and self-expression in your life. Each crystal embodies a certain purpose that is just for you, and channels more energy for you to use.

As this takes effect, you will discover more things about yourself and move toward other realizations. Write down these realizations and journal about what they mean to you, and how they have changed your outlook.

Your crystal code is not a static formula; it is dynamic and ever changing. As time goes by, you may find that you wish to change one or more of your crystals; this is fine (although it is best not to change your crystals too frequently or abruptly). Apply your crystal code to all life situations and discover your path to personal fulfilment.

Please remember that although there are many instructions given in this book, nothing can take the place of your intuition. If you feel strongly that a crystal has a specific effect, then that is very probably correct, at least for you. You should be guided by your intuition primarily – never tell yourself you must be wrong because of something you read in a book.

For each of the following chapters, a selection of 12 crystals has been suggested from which you may choose. These crystals are listed for their particular properties, each offering something different but suitable to the purpose. Experiment with each one whenever you feel drawn to it. However, if you feel that none of the crystals listed is correct, and you wish to choose something completely different, then you should follow your own inner convictions.

OBTAINING AND CHOOSING CRYSTALS

It has never been easier to obtain crystals – many New Age and knick-knack shops sell an array of tumble-stones (crystals that have been ground mechanically to create a smooth finish) for very little money. There are an increasing number of specialist stores solely devoted to selling lovely crystals in all shapes and sizes – as ornaments, jewellery or aids to meditation and esoteric practices.

If you have only recently become interested in crystals, allow yourself the time to collect the ones that you like, handling them, arranging them and playing with them. You may start to pick up impressions from them or feel that certain crystals have certain effects.

In each of the following chapters, you will be given methods for choosing the crystal that relates to the area of life in question – love, money or relaxation, for example. These methods involve accessing your intuition. However, when you are choosing crystals in a shop, you will not be able to perform these exercises, so you need to learn to listen to the "call" of a crystal. Many people believe that crystals choose them. I vividly remember the evening when a heart-shaped piece of green tourmaline insisted from across the room that I buy it. It has been with me ever since, and is beside me as I write.

When choosing a crystal, learn to listen to your body. A crystal that is right for you may give you a sensation in the pit of your stomach, in your heart or in your head. You may feel tingling, you may even "taste" the crystal. You may think you hear music or your eye may simply be drawn to a specific crystal. If you are not sure, relax and see what comes to mind. Hold the crystal in your palm and see what impressions you get. Or you may just know that you want a certain crystal. The ability to choose crystals may require practice, but remember you can't really get it wrong. Any crystal may be right, but some will be more right than others. It is best to store crystals away from the light, wrapped in black velvet, especially if you are keeping them to use in specific exercises and rituals.

CLEANSING YOUR CRYSTALS

All crystals, whether tumble-stones, crystal balls, healing wands or jewellery, should be cleansed before using or wearing because crystals pick up and absorb influences. Some people believe that some crystals never need cleansing (citrine, for instance) but it can never do any harm to cleanse a crystal, even if all that needs removing are the most superficial influences of someone else's touch. Be especially careful of crystals that have been used by another person for esoteric purposes or have been worn on the body; cleanse these thoroughly before using them.

Crystals are very delicate and should be treated with great care when cleansing. Tumble-stones are tougher, because they have been ground to a smooth and durable finish, but they still need respect. Basically, what cleanses your crystal is your intention to do so. If you are good at visualizing, place your crystal in front of you on a white cloth, and simply imagine a stream of pure water flowing through the crystal, deeply cleansing it. Do this visualization for as long as you feel necessary, and then a little longer.

If you want to do something more physical, take your crystal to a stream and hold it in the water, while affirming that all impurities are being removed. Or you may soak your crystal overnight in spring water. Never use salt water, as it can damage some crystals, and be aware that some crystals, such as selenite, are water-soluble and so should never be cleansed by this method. Crystals should be allowed to dry naturally on a clean cloth; do not rub them. Crystals should be cleansed each time you use them, before being safely put away until next time.

You can also clean crystals by passing them through incense smoke; a lavender joss stick will serve this purpose admirably. Passing them through (or near) a candle flame will also do the trick. Another method suggests leaving your crystal in an earthenware bowl of unrefined brown rice overnight. The rice should be thrown away after this and not eaten.

CHARGING YOUR CRYSTALS

After choosing and cleansing your crystals, you will want to charge them up with your own essence to make them truly "yours". You may do this simply by holding the crystal between your palms and sending energy into it, visualizing the crystal pulsating with the life force that you have imparted.

Alternatively, you may wish to perform a small ritual charge and also dedicate your crystal to divine powers. You will need a candle, a stone, a lavender joss stick and a glass with a stem (such as a wine glass) containing water. If you have a statue of a goddess or god that is meaningful to you, have this close by. You will also need your crystal.

Affirm that your ritual space is clear. Sweep it with a broom or duster as a symbol of cleansing. Imagine a protective circle surrounding you. Place the stone roughly to your north, the joss stick to the east, the candle to the south and the glass of water to the west. If you live in the southern hemisphere, reverse the positions of the candle and stone. These objects represent the four elements – earth, fire, air and water – and the directions to which they have a time-honoured link in esoteric tradition. Place your statue by the element you prefer.

Holding your crystal in your hand, face the stone and say: "I dedicate this crystal to the powers of earth, for grounding and protection." Move sun-wise (clockwise in the northern hemisphere, anticlockwise in the south) visiting the other elements. Face the joss stick and say: "I dedicate this crystal to the powers of air, for clarity and truth." Face the candle and say: "I dedicate this crystal to the powers of fire, for courage and energy." Finally, face the glass and say: "I dedicate this crystal to the powers of water, for healing and purity."

Now your crystal is truly charged up. Mentally dismantle your protective circle and store your crystal with care.

COLOURS AND SHAPES

Crystals come in all the colours of the rainbow, and the colour of a crystal reveals something of its nature. For instance, a red crystal brings with it energy, vitality and passion, a purple one is spiritual and uplifting while a green crystal may resonate more with earthly matters, such as creativity, money and plants. However, you will find a variety of colours included in each section, to give a different nuance of meaning. Amethyst and clear quartz may have a more obvious connection to higher states, but if you are into nature mysticism, then green agate may suit you, and if you seek tantric bliss, rhodocrosite could be a better companion. It is your choice.

Crystals come in many different shapes, but for the purposes of this book we are mainly concentrating on tumble-stones, as these are cheaper and easier to handle. Crystals not available as tumble-stones should be purchased as a very small piece. However, in the case of certain special crystals it is a good idea to obtain them in other shapes – for instance, a quartz wand is invaluable for healing, and scrying is best done with a crystal in the traditional ball shape.

YOUR PERSONALITY CRYSTAL

Perhaps the most important of your crystal choices is your Personality Crystal. Not only is it an expression of the real "you", but it also represents your potential as a person.

The interpretation of your choice of crystal may surprise you by describing qualities you did not know you possessed, or it may seem immediately "right". Either way, your Personality Crystal is there to empower you and help you to become the person you are destined to be.

It is worthwhile investing in all of the listed crystals as tumble-stones, not only to make choosing easier and because they are inexpensive, but because at a later date you may want to reselect your Personality Crystal. As we go through life, we change. Sometimes, however, this change may take place at a profound level.

It is as if we have found another layer to our personality, or possibly as if there was another person within who has now found the light of day. This shows that we are developing as human beings.

Your Personality Crystal should facilitate this change, as you fully express that facet of your personality represented by the crystal. If and when it is appropriate, you will be able to move on. And should you wish to return to a previous crystal, that is fine too. It doesn't signify a backward step, but merely a return at a new level of experience.

CHOOSING YOUR PERSONALITY CRYSTAL

Your Personality Crystal is so special that you may not feel that you need to make any effort to "choose". You may feel immediately drawn to a crystal, or you may have loved this particular stone for some time. But if you need a little help or want to make sure, try one of the following methods. Use the spaces provided to note down your experiences as you make this choice.

YOU WILL NEED

Tumble-stones of the following crystals:
garnet, green tourmaline, citrine, moonstone, sunstone, moss agate, blue quartz, bloodstone, ametrine, onyx, aquamarine and labradorite

(or the name of the crystal written on paper.)

Gold candle; oils or joss sticks of frankincense or cinnamon; gold cloth.

Before you begin any of the rituals, do you feel drawn to any of the crystals in front of you? If you do, does your reaction feel emotional, intellectual or physical?

....
....
....
....
....
....
....
....
....
....
....
....

THE CLOTH BAG METHOD

Place all the crystals or their substitutes in a cloth bag | Sit quietly with your eyes closed and relax | Be aware of your body | Let a sensation of warmth spread through you, starting as a golden glow behind your navel, gradually energizing your entire body | When you feel ready, reach into the bag and choose your stone | Visualize the glow receding back behind your navel and closing off.

What thoughts came to you as you held the bag, and then as you reached into it? Which crystal did you choose? Did you "see", "feel" or "hear" it during the process? If you did, what did it "look", "feel" or "sound" like?

....

....

....

....

....

....

....

....

....

....

....

....

....

....

....

....

THE VISUALIZATION METHOD ONE

Place all the crystals in front of you with a gold candle behind them |
Burn a joss stick of frankincense or cinnamon, or heat either of those
oils in an oil burner | Light the gold candle behind the crystals | Sit in
front of the crystals and think about all that makes you "you".

What do you like about yourself? What are you good
at? How would you describe yourself? How have friends
described you, and what qualities have they seen in you?
And what would you like to be like?

....

....

....

....

....

....

....

....

....

....

....

....

....

....

Now open your eyes. Which crystal are you drawn to? Which seems to
ask to be picked up? That is your Personality Crystal. If you are
undecided, take away those you feel sure are not right for you, and
repeat the exercise until you have eliminated all but one.

THE CRYSTAL CIRCLE METHOD

Place your crystals in a circle on a gold cloth | In the centre of the circle, place a large golden candle | Around the candle, place articles that are personal and precious to you – choose things that are about you as a person, not about someone or something else | For instance, a wedding or engagement ring is about your relationship, and your purse is about money, but your diary or any article you acquired simply because you loved it are truer expressions of yourself | Light the candle and burn incense as you did for the visualization method | Relax and become steady and calm | Start to focus on the crystals.

Which crystal do you feel should join your special possessions around the candle? Perhaps the candlelight glints on one crystal more brightly than on the others. Maybe you feel more drawn to one crystal. Perhaps one of the crystals feels like "home" to you, and feels like it belongs with your other personal items.
Write about it here.

....

....

....

....

....

....

....

....

....

....

....

....

THE VISUALIZATION METHOD TWO

Lay the crystals out and burn a candle and some incense as for the visualization method | Let yourself be calm and peaceful | Cast your mind back to a time when you felt particularly happy, complete, fulfilled and recognized (or just one or two of those descriptions).

Which crystal seems the best expression of that time? Does one of them feel like it belongs in that moment with you? Perhaps one of the crystals seems to hold the energy of that time when you felt fulfilled. How do you know which crystal it is? Does it seem to shine more brightly as you visualize? Or perhaps you can "hear" it connecting with that happy memory?

....

....

....

....

....

....

....

....

....

....

....

....

....

Sometimes you may find that several crystals seem to respond to your happy thoughts. If so, narrow down your choice with successive attempts until you are left with the one that responds most strongly. This crystal is your best choice.

Which method did you choose to help you find your
Personality Crystal, and why did you feel drawn to that
method? How did you feel before you started the process
– nervous, excited? And how do you feel about the crystal
you have chosen? Is it the one you expected?

....

....

....

....

....

....

....

....

....

....

....

....

....

....

....

....

....

....

....

....

....

....

....

INTERPRETING YOUR PERSONALITY CRYSTAL

This section offers interpretations of each of the Personality Crystals. Use the journal spaces to reflect on how the crystal may be guiding you toward rethinking or re-evaluating aspects of your personality. Are your needs being met? And, if they're not, what is stopping this? Now that you've chosen your Personality Crystal, what do you think it can teach you?

BLOODSTONE

Intense and passionate, you love and hate with equal strength. You find it hard to forgive and forget. However, for a true friend you are prepared to "walk through the shadow of the valley of death". Your courage and determination are unbeatable and you are generous with your help and sympathy, although you prefer to help those who also help themselves. Knowledge is power and you like to get to the bottom of things.

In relationships, once you give your heart, it is given for good, and you can be jealous as well as deeply empathic. It is important for you to have periods alone in order to regenerate yourself.

You are often best at behind-the-scenes work, using your DEDUCTIVE abilities, but you can also be DRAMATIC and ARTISTIC.

....
....
....
....
....
....
....
....
....
....

CITRINE

You are a dynamic, lively person with a smile on your face. Your mind is always active; you have a hunger for knowledge, but require more than just facts. It is important for you to have your powers of reason stimulated and to be able to come to your own conclusions. You love to communicate; whether this is about deep matters or some entertaining gossip, you can be very witty.

In relationships, mental rapport is essential to you, along with shared cultural interests. A great flirt, you are not too eager to commit yourself and often change your mind. Be careful not to be too "in the head" – gut feelings and emotions are just as important as ideas.

Professions such as PUBLISHING and the MEDIA may appeal and your INGENUITY can take you far in life.

. . . .
. . . .
. . . .
. . . .
. . . .
. . . .
. . . .
. . . .
. . . .
. . . .
. . . .
. . . .
. . . .
. . . .
. . . .
. . . .

ONYX

Practical and restrained, you value common sense and security, and like to feel you are progressing steadily in life. It is important to you to be in control of as many things as possible – like the Boy Scouts, your motto is "Be prepared". You can be pessimistic and may erect barriers in life by trying to be one step ahead.

In relationships you tend to be reserved; you do not like to give too much away about your feelings and sometimes you are not sure what they are. Once you decide someone is suitable for you, however, you support that person in all ways and you are a committed family member.

You work best where your PLANNING and CONSTRUCTING abilities are utilized; you are capable of PATIENCE in achieving long-term goals.

. . . .
. . . .
. . . .
. . . .
. . . .
. . . .
. . . .
. . . .
. . . .
. . . .
. . . .

GARNET

You are an energetic and enterprising person, sometimes jumping in where angels fear to tread. Patience is not your virtue, and you often lose interest in things that take too long.

A person of initiative and ideas, you prefer to sow rather than to stay around and reap. You have great courage and leadership qualities and you take a positive attitude to life, although when things do not go your way, you can sometimes become angry and moody.

Prepared to stick up for yourself and your friends where necessary, you can be bossy and aggressive, but also generous, responsible and good at organizing. Don't worry if some say you are self-important: always keep things in proportion and remain effective.

You work best where your DRIVE and MANAGERIAL talents can have full scope and where you can take the INITIATIVE.

GREEN TOURMALINE

You are patient and persevering. You love stability and security, and you do your best to create this around you. Practical things such as money and creature comforts are important. You take a realistic, pragmatic approach to life, preferring to believe the evidence of your senses, although you are aware of ambience and love peace.

Affectionate, kind and dependable, you can be very stubborn and resistant to anything new. What's yours is yours and you can be possessive, but you will offer help to those you love.

You are probably good at gardening, having an affinity with growing things, and you are drawn to all forms of pleasure and life's bounty.

You love CREATIVE pursuits and are at your best in any profession that offers you STABILITY, COMFORT, good pay and an outlet for your ARTISTIC talents.

....
....
....
....
....
....
....
....
....
....
....
....
....
....
....

LABRADORITE

Imaginative and mystical, sometimes it seems you are closer to the world of the spirit than to this world. You are a deeply sympathetic and empathic individual, feeling the ills of others as if they were your own. You need to protect yourself from too many demands, since you find it hard to say "no". Change is your middle name, since you see so many sides to everything that it is impossible to find one way of being, one point of view that fits everything.

Your emotions are very strong and you tend to go through life being in love with a person or thing. Artistic and creative, you often find it hard to stick to one thing, being easily distracted. You are very idealistic and sensitive, and you need time on your own to help you recharge your batteries. Follow your dreams and keep your feet on the ground.

You prefer to be INDEPENDENT in your work, but you need to know that it is MEANINGFUL and/or CREATIVE.

....
....
....
....
....
....
....
....
....
....
....
....
....
....
....

MOONSTONE

Your emotions and instincts are very strong, making you extremely protective of yourself and those whom you love. Home and family are central to your existence and you are a nurturing, supportive person. However, you can also be touchy and moody – if someone hurts you, this may never be forgotten, for your memory is excellent.

Your dreams are very important to you and you are very intuitive, but you are also practical, managing money wisely and able to sense whom you can trust. Closeness and empathy are vital and you need to feel loved and understood. It is very hard for you to let go of the past and anything that represents it, so you can be an indiscriminate hoarder.

You function best when your sympathetic, CARING nature is valued, where your TENACITY is respected and your PRIVACY is not invaded.

....
....
....
....
....
....
....

....
....
....
....
....
....
....
....

MOSS AGATE

Refined and discriminating, you have the instincts of an epicure. No detail passes you by and you are an excellent organizer. Able to get to the root of most things, you are a "fixer", practical, tidy and thorough. Being useful is important to you and you are happiest when busy and needed by others.

You can be modest and self-effacing, although if you are taken for granted this makes you unhappy. You are your own worst critic and therefore all the more sensitive to criticism from others, although you are very aware of the shortcomings of other people. Sometimes you favour a hands-on approach and you can achieve wonderful things in the garden, kitchen and office, as long as you relax.

Your HIGH STANDARDS, EFFICIENCY and passion for EXCELLENCE need to find expression in your work.

....
....
....
....
....
....
....
....
....
....
....
....
....

and you can be inconsiderate, reckless and tactless – but you are nonetheless warm-hearted.

You function best where your ENERGY and ENTHUSIASM can have full rein and where you can ENCOURAGE others to appreciate life.

....
....
....
....
....
....
....
....
....
....
....
....
....
....

AMETRINE

You are adventurous and far-seeing, often so preoccupied with possibilities and philosophies that you may not see what is under your nose. Freedom is very important to you, and you probably like to travel, either literally or mentally. You seek always to expand your experience and education, learning about foreign cultures and religions, bringing what they have to offer into your own life and using it enthusiastically.

Usually optimistic and generous, you take a positive attitude to life and encourage others to do the same. Sometimes you can be careless because your mind is far away,

AQUAMARINE

Being an individual is the most important thing to you, and you tend to live your life to the beat of a "different drum". Although you like to have a wide circle of friends, you are not eager to let anyone too close because this could cramp your style.

Highly original, inventive and even rebellious at times, you pursue your own ideals, for these are the stuff of life to you.

You may change your mind a hundred times, but no one will change it for you, and sometimes you can be eccentric, stubborn and awkward. Although you may be very intellectual, you hate being cooped up at a desk. You seek the truth and are very concerned with the welfare of humans, animals and the planet itself, so you may be involved with charitable concerns.

You need to be where you can be FREE and independent and where there is scope for your RESOURCEFULNESS and UNIQUE perspective.

....
....
....
....
....
....
....
....
....
....
....
....
....
....
....
....
....
....

SUNSTONE

Your main drive in life is to shine as brightly as you can wherever you are, whatever you are doing. Proud and dignified, you are usually well respected for your reliability, generosity and the strength of your personality. Your faith in life is considerable and your attitude is noble to the point that you often miss small details.

Because you are very idealistic and honest, you can be very hurt when others let you down. Although you are magnanimous, joyful and loving, you can also be a little bossy and conceited on occasion, and sometimes you show off.

You function best where there is plenty of scope for your sense of drama; you like to bask in the LIMELIGHT and use your AUTHORITY, and can be good at MANAGING large-scale projects.

....
....
....
....
....
....
....
....
....
....

....
....
....
....
....
....
....
....
....
....
....
....
....
....
....
....
....

BLUE QUARTZ

Beautiful surroundings and a peaceful
atmosphere are as necessary to you as the
air you breathe and you do your best to
please everyone. In fact, it is often hard for
you to make up your mind as you try to fit
in with both sides. However, while you
may appear pliable and biddable, you have
a laser-sharp brain and anyone who tries
to take advantage of you sooner or later
finds themselves gently, firmly and
cleverly put in their place!

Tactful and gracious, you probably have
wonderful manners and dress sense.
Sometimes, however, you can be lazy and
procrastinating, a quiet life being the most
important thing on your agenda along with
regular retail therapy. You cannot function
where there is ugliness and discord.

You should seek a place where your
TALENT for DIPLOMACY and your eye for
what is lovely are APPRECIATED.

PERSONALITY RITUALS

The following pages contain rituals, meditations
and visualizations for you to practise with your
Personality Crystal.

Working with your Personality Crystal helps you develop
a deeper understanding of your own energies, and helps
you to connect with and develop the aspects of your
personality that are most important to you.

Use the journal spaces to record your
experiences of these rituals.

PERSONALITY PLUS VISUALIZATION

Your crystal can help you shine in life by focusing your own special talents and energies. Because your Personality Crystal is a concentration of your own energies, it can serve to intensify your best and strongest characteristics. Try this simple visualization when you have to speak in public or on the first day of a new job – or whenever you need to feel special and empowered.

1. Lie down comfortably in a dimly lit room. Relax and place your crystal on your navel. Imagine that the crystal is starting to glow brighter and brighter. Feel the radiance within your body – beautiful, warming, exciting. Enjoy the feeling.

2. Now imagine an answering glow from behind your navel combining with that of the crystal so that you are suffused with brilliance. Visualize the light growing and extending, encircling you in an egg shape. When you are ready, visualize yourself in the coming situation, but doing it wonderfully, feeling truly uplifted and pleased with yourself. Hold this visualization as long as you can.

3. When you are ready, come back to ordinary awareness. Pat your body to make sure you are properly grounded. Be sure to take the crystal with you when you face the challenge.

What was this experience like for you? How did you feel about the situation you are preparing for before you carried out this ritual? And how do you feel about it now?

....
....
....
....
....
....
....
....
....
....
....
....
....
....

SELF-DEVELOPMENT VISUALIZATION

Taking the time to reflect on your development with your Personality Crystal can be deeply rewarding.

1. Lie down where you won't be disturbed and relax deeply. Holding your crystal in one of your palms, let your mind drift. Imagine walking down a narrow country road. Look around and notice the trees and fields, the green of the plants, the blue of the sky. Listen to the sounds, be aware of the sun on your skin, the breeze in your hair. Feel your feet making solid contact with the ground – really be there.

2. You now come to a crossroads. One path leads up a hill – the road bends and twists so you cannot see along it but you can spot in the distance that it eventually leads high up a steep and rocky slope. Another path leads deep into the darkness of a forest and another down to a lake. Which one should you take?

3. Now be aware that a spirit is materializing from your crystal and holding your hand. Take the trouble to visualize your crystal spirit. Commune if you wish.

4. The spirit of your crystal will now lead you down one of the paths. Be assured that you are safe with your crystal spirit. All that you see now is personal to you. Explore but do not jump to conclusions.

5. When you are ready, thank the crystal spirit, say goodbye and come back to everyday awareness, pat your body and drink some water to ground yourself.

Write down all you remember. What did your crystal spirit look, sound and feel like? What did your experience convey about your development?

....
....
....
....
....
....
....
....
....
....
....
....
....

WEARING YOUR CRYSTAL

More than any of your other crystals, you will want to wear your Personality Crystal to enhance your special qualities and to feel powerful. Your crystal has a slightly different effect according to which part of the body it is adorning.

Necklace: This stimulates your ability to express yourself verbally, which is excellent for any form of speaking, negotiating, communicating or talking at parties.

Pendant: Worn near your heart, it stimulates your sympathetic responses to people you meet, enabling you to make a strong impression.

Earrings: Your ears are attuned to anything that can enhance your feeling of "specialness" such as compliments and heightened understanding.

Nose stud: Gives you an instinct for being in the right place at the right time.

Navel stud: Enhances your personal power, although navel piercings are not popular with acupuncturists as the navel is on an important meridian and interfering with it could cause depression, so be aware.

Finger ring: Your creativity and effectiveness will be increased by wearing your crystal on your hand: index finger – leadership; second finger – practical and enduring achievement; third finger – artistic endeavour; little finger – writing and communication; thumb –

independence. The meanings are more receptive than active in your least dominant hand; in a right-handed person the third finger of the left hand relates more to appreciating the beautiful than actually creating it.

Bracelet: Increases your openness to opportunities and your ability to seize them.

Anklet: Gives you the confidence to explore and to draw from your experiences all that can help you grow and develop.

Toe ring: Takes you on wonderful adventures to discover many things about yourself.

YOUR
RELAXATION
CRYSTAL

Your Relaxation Crystal will help you to unwind in the
way best suited to you. However, it is asking a lot of
your crystal to expect it to teach you how to relax if
you are used to being uptight!

In order to be able to tune in to your Relaxation Crystal enough to choose the one that is right for you, it may be necessary to learn the basics of relaxation. This will stand you in good stead for many of the exercises in this book and will be a great help when you meditate.

All manner of serious physical ailments, such as stroke and heart disease, are linked to stress. Stress depresses the immune system and can result in many things, from recurrent infections to painful migraines.

Relaxation, as we are coming to understand, is vital to our health. It is also vital to the expansion of consciousness. Tension is the one major barrier that comes between you and your intuition, your inner wisdom and your capacity for true joy. Learning to relax in body and mind is a skill that most of us in the West need to learn.

Let us begin.

PRACTISING YOUR RELAXATION TECHNIQUE

Your unconscious mind is like a child, and, child-like, it responds best to routine. Once your unconscious has learned the principles of relaxation it will become automatic. Channels are then opened both for creative playfulness and also for the transmission of inspiration.

Begin your relaxation practice by deciding on a time of day when you are able to relax for ten minutes. This needs to be done every day! If you miss one day out of seven, this is not the end of the world, but if you miss it right at the beginning, it will take longer to establish your pattern. Relaxing once a week for an hour is certainly no substitute, although it may be better than nothing; most likely you will find that it is not possible and will either fall asleep or find yourself mulling over your problems.

1. If you are an early bird, the morning may be the best time to begin. Get ready for the day ten minutes earlier and settle for your relaxation. Children and pets should be kept out. Turn your phone onto silent mode. Lie on your bed, because that says 'relax!' to your unconscious. (If you feel like you may fall asleep, you may need to adopt a more alert position, such as sitting up in a chair or sitting cross-legged on the floor). Lavender oil heated in a burner or placed on your temples can help, and/or you may want to play soft music. A relaxing tea such as camomile can also help if you tend to be anxious.

2. Bring your consciousness into your body and be very aware of your comfort. Count yourself in by saying: 'One, relax, two, relax, three, relax.' Focus on your feet, feeling all the muscles in them, tensing them slightly and then relaxing. This process of tensing makes you aware of your muscles and helps you to relax them. Now move on up your legs, tensing and relaxing, then focus on your pelvis, buttocks, internal muscles, abdomen, back, chest and shoulders – pay special attention to this prime tension site. Travel all the way down your arms, into your fingers, clenching your fists and relaxing. Finally, the myriad muscles in your neck, jaw, face and scalp need the screw-up-and-relax routine.

3. Once you are relaxed, visualize yourself somewhere very pleasant. Concentrate on what you see, hear, smell and touch – do not be distracted into imagining scenarios, however pleasant, and don't allow yourself to get drawn into memories. If you begin to do this, pull back into your body and do a quick relaxation check before taking yourself back to your beautiful place. At the end of your relaxation, count yourself back up by saying, 'Three, two, one, awaken.' Consciously ground yourself by patting your body or eating and drinking something.

How did you feel before you started this relaxation exercise, and how do you feel now? Rested, energized, sleepy? Describe the beautiful place you vizualised, remembering to note as many details as you can.

....

....

....

....

....

....

....

....

....

....

....

....

....

....

....

....

....

....

CHOOSING YOUR RELAXATION CRYSTAL

When you are reasonably good at relaxing, you can choose your crystal. Naturally you will be impatient, but try to allow two weeks of regular relaxation before making your selection, if you can. If you cannot wait, it is not the end of the world, for none of the crystals will hinder you. However, you may want to revisit this at a later date as you may choose differently. Use the spaces provided to note down your experiences in making this choice.

YOU WILL NEED

Choose from:
rose quartz, sugilite, lepidolite, aquamarine, gold calcite, pink chalcedony, aragonite, blue tourmaline, smithsonite, rhodochrosite, prehnite and red jasper.

Before you begin, do you feel particularly drawn to any of the crystals in front of you? Do any seem to invoke a sense of calm and peace?

....
....
....
....
....
....
....
....
....
....
....
....
....
....

RELAXATION METHOD ONE

Set out all the crystals (or you can use pictures or their names written on slips of paper) close to you when you are relaxing | Go into your relaxation routine as outlined on the previous page and concentrate totally on your body | Then go to your pleasant place | At this point, you may get a vivid sense of which crystal to choose | If so, go with this choice.

Did you get a sense of the right crystal while you were in your pleasant place? What was it like?

....

....

....

RELAXATION METHOD TWO

Begin the relaxation routine as outlined above and go to your pleasant place | Continue with your relaxation in the same way as normal and come back to everyday awakening when you are ready | When you come out of your relaxation, but before grounding yourself, ask yourself which crystal "feels right" | A crystal may occur to you at this point: this is your Relaxation Crystal.

Which crystal did you choose?
What made you choose it?

....

....

....

Your crystal will help you relax in any way you wish, whether this is by going more deeply into states of meditation or by more active methods such as art, creativity, play or sport.

INTERPRETING YOUR RELAXATION CRYSTAL

Here, you can learn a bit more about your Relaxation Crystal. Everyone relaxes differently, so think about what relaxation means to you and then look at the interpretations below. Use the spaces to journal about how your new Relaxation Crystal ties in with your own personal ways of unwinding.

AQUAMARINE

This wonderful stone is for people who are over-sensitive; it calms their fears, helping them to get things into perspective and to use, in a positive manner, the information their almost-psychic senses acquire. If you have chosen this stone, you may need its soothing influence, especially to bring something troublesome to a satisfactory end, so that you can relax and get on with your life.

If you feel burdened by responsibility, aquamarine will help you to cope and feel worthwhile. On a physical note, if your favourite form of recreation is a watersport such as boating, swimming or diving, then traditionally this is the perfect stone to wear, both to keep you safe and to attune you to the relaxing blessings of water.

Aquamarine can also get you out of a boring RUT by WIDENING your PERSPECTIVE.

....
....
....
....
....
....
....
....
....
....
....
....
....
....
....
....
....
....

ARAGONITE

If you have chosen this crystal then the chances are that physical relaxation is of paramount importance to you and you want to feel comfortable in your body. Possibly, you are a sensuous person and make judgements on the basis of practicality, or it may also be that your intuition expresses itself physically, as in "gut feelings" and the like. At the other extreme, if you have become "spaced out", aragonite will bring you firmly and reassuringly back to the here and now.

Aragonite warms the body and helps with conditions such as restless legs. If you push yourself too hard at work, aragonite reminds you to ease up and nurture yourself; it is a great friend if cooking is your hobby.

It teaches you that your BODY is the TEMPLE of your SOUL and that respect for its needs is essential to all occupations and enjoyment.

....

....

....

....

....

....

....

....

....

....

GOLD CALCITE

Gold calcite drives away the cobwebs and brings a breath of fresh air into your life. If you have become a bit of a couch potato you may choose gold calcite to get you moving, and so experience the relaxing benefits of exercise, possibly in the open air. Gold calcite will also attract you if you are already active, but want to develop this.

It clears the mind, enabling you to make intelligent choices about your leisure. It is excellent for sharpening the brain if you like crosswords and puzzles. It is hard to feel despondent with this stone close by. Gold calcite inspires a sense of possibilities and is a great motivator.

It is a great stone to keep you CALM and FOCUSED when STUDYING and so will help you choose the correct evening class and keep at it.

....

....

....

....
....
....
....
....
....
....
....
....
....
....
....
....

helped by pink chalcedony. This stone gently encourages you to try new things, having faith in the bounty of the world to bring you enjoyment.

One of its gifts is to STOP you worrying about your health and to EASE psychosomatic SYMPTOMS.

....
....
....
....
....
....
....
....
....
....
....
....

PINK CHALCEDONY

If you enjoy recreation with a group of friends, chalcedony will help retain harmony and cooperation. This is a stone for happiness and goodwill.

If you have been troubled by nightmares, pink chalcedony will take you to a deeper level of relaxation, where you are in contact only with peaceful realms and so experience regenerating sleep.

Pink chalcedony will keep you aware of the magic in the world and help you to enjoy fantasy and stories. It is a great companion if you enjoy novels but may also inspire you to entertain others. Reading aloud is

RED JASPER

Red jasper gives a boost to your get-up-and-go. It is a great stone to choose if you love sports because it will give you determination and staying power, and that competitive edge. However, this is very much an aid to relaxation and recreation, for it takes you out of your routine so that you can forget about stresses and cares while you do something active.

If you are convalescing following illness or surgery, red jasper will enable you to rest and build up your reserves of strength. This is a stone of power, energy and true recreation.

And if you unwind best of all with some "horizontal action", red jasper will STIMULATE your SEX-DRIVE, as well as helping you to TUNE in to your lover.

....
....
....
....
....
....
....
....
....
....
....
....
....

LEPIDOLITE

If you tend to go to extremes, lepidolite is a wonderful stabilizer, calming you when you are "hyper" and encouraging you when you feel depressed. If you want to be comfortable alone, to feel the peace of your own space, this stone is for you. If you are harassed and wish to make the most of any tranquil interludes, lepidolite will help you to move smoothly into a state of calm.

It is useful for relieving the stresses of daily life and will enable you to let go of anger and frustration. You may have chosen it instinctively if you are subject to harmful emotions such as hatred (of your co-worker, for instance) or road rage. It relieves nightmares and aids psychic powers.

If you love to use your leisure time READING TAROT or doing ASTROLOGY, lepidolite is a fine companion.

....
....
....
....
....
....
....
....
....
....
....
....
....
....
....
....

PREHNITE

If you have chosen prehnite, you feel a need to change your perspective, to have a wider view of reality than the one you may feel stuck with, and to plug into a more "cosmic consciousness". Prehnite enhances love of Nature and the ability to use its healing influence. On a practical level, prehnite helps you to get rid of the junk that may be crowding your life and to have faith that the Universe will provide you with what you need.

Keep it by you when sorting and recycling, for a wonderful feeling of freedom. It also helps you organize your domestic space, so that harmony prevails and it becomes a haven of healing for you and your family.

This stone also CALMS irrational FEARS and HYPERACTIVITY.

....
....
....
....
....
....
....
....
....
....

....
....
....
....

RHODOCHROSITE

This dynamic stone is a wonderful support and encouragement if you like to spend your spare time in charitable pursuits. It is positive and creative, inspiring resourceful solutions and leading to delight.

Rhodochrosite will help you laugh and be warm and playful. It is a sexy stone, helping you to connect with your lover and be honest about your needs, teaching you that all your feelings are acceptable.

This is not an especially "polite" stone, because it frees up feelings and encourages honesty, so if you are prone to use your spare time pleasing others, rhodochrosite will enable you to say "no" pleasantly and firmly.

It is also a fine stone for any CREATIVE work such as arts and crafts, sculpture or anything that requires you to be PASSIONATE and FULL-BLOODED.

....
....
....
....

....
....
....
....
....
....
....
....
....
....
....

ensure that you seek the company of warm and loving souls.

It will guide you to CHOOSE CLOTHES and adornments, to make you look your BEST.

....
....
....
....
....
....
....
....
....
....
....

ROSE QUARTZ

If you have chosen rose quartz then relaxation, to you, means closeness with friends and family or romantic times with a lover. This stone will bring calm in a family crisis or in traumatic times, and it will enable you to appreciate beauty in your surroundings and in other people. It will also enhance your response to art and music.

If you have been hurt and are plagued by resentment and/or jealousy, gentle rose quartz will enable you to let go of those negative feelings, to feel warmth and affection and to prepare yourself to love again. Most important of all, rose quartz teaches you to love yourself, to count all your good qualities and to

SMITHSONITE

Should you feel close to a breakdown, soothing smithsonite will help you to let go of tension and smile. If you want to relax well in the company of children, this stone will help you to relate to them by putting you in touch with your own "inner child". It helps you to see the ways in which your inner child may be hurt and needy, and to heal this without detriment to your relationships with others.

Life's problems seem at a distance with smithsonite; it allows you to get things into perspective. It will also help you to be tactful and to get your own way by diplomacy, so if you have a leadership role in a club, smithsonite might be your choice to oil the wheels – and get your way!

Placed beneath the bed, smithsonite BOOSTS the IMMUNE system and COMBATS alcoholism.

....
....
....
....
....
....
....
....
....
....
....
....
....
....
....
....
....
....
....

SUGILITE

If your work involves healing and helping people, sugilite will help you to remain positive while keeping a sense of vocation and purpose. It brings you the peace of knowing that you act by your convictions, and the relaxation in the knowledge of a benign and meaningful Universe. It is an extremely spiritual stone, bringing enlightenment and inspiration if you feel you are on an inner quest or wish to deepen your experience.

If you have been traumatized or let down, sugilite brings calm, comfort and hope. It also helps with special needs such as autism or dyslexia by connecting to the deep areas where such problems arise. If you have chosen sugilite, you may see relaxation in terms of self-development and spiritual progress. It is also good for pain relief, especially if you have a headache.

This stone will help you to OPEN out to the TRUE MEANINGS in your life.

....
....
....
....
....
....

....
....
....
....
....
....
....
....
....
....
....

On a practical note, tourmaline helps you be physically COORDINATED and so SUPPORTS many ACTIVITIES, from writing to table tennis.

....
....
....
....
....
....
....
....
....
....
....
....
....
....
....
....
....

BLUE TOURMALINE

This is an excellent stone for communication, so if you feel uptight when trying to express yourself or have a special difficulty such as a stammer, blue tourmaline will help you relax and let the words flow. Along with green tourmaline, it helps you to feel in tune with plants and is wonderful if gardening, or anything to do with growth, is your hobby.

If you like to use your spare time helping the environment, this stone will show you the way. If you have chosen blue tourmaline, you may have a pent-up unhappiness that you need to release, or you may be helping others to do this. It is a lovely "tea and sympathy" stone.

RELAXATION RITUALS

The following pages contain rituals, meditations and visualizations for you to practise with your Relaxation Crystal.

Working with your Relaxation Crystal will help you focus your energies on achieving a sense of peace and calm.

Use the journal spaces to record how you feel during and after these exercises. If you do achieve a feeling of relaxation, write about how long that lasts and whether you can carry it with you throughout your day.

FREE YOUR MIND VISUALIZATION

Many of the restrictions we experience in life are self-imposed. This visualization will help you to get a wider perspective.

1. Sit or lie comfortably and relax as described at the beginning of the chapter. Hold your Relaxation Crystal cupped in your palms or, if you are lying down, place it on your solar plexus with your hands gently covering it. Imagine that your crystal is radiating a force field. You may experience a tingling in your hands and body as you do this. Feel this force field forming a bubble around you. You are becoming weightless. Visualize yourself rising into the air, up and up, higher and higher.

2. Now you are drifting away, leaving behind your house and street, out over the open country. Green fields stretch beneath you, meandering rivers, woodland, hills, valleys, mountain and lakes. Drink in the colours and the landscapes.

3. Now you are drifting out over the ocean. Beneath you, the waves heave, blue, grey, emerald, purple. There is only water, deep peaceful water. Dusk begins to fall and the full moon appears. How marvellously it reflects on the water. You feel yourself going up higher, into the indigo sky spattered with stars and luminous with moonlight.

4. You are leaving the Earth behind. There it hangs in space, a beautiful emerald orb with the moon beside it. In the distance the sun is getting smaller as you drift into the dark reaches of the solar system. Around you there are stars shining like crystals. Travel as long and as far as you like and when you are ready to come back to everyday awareness, ground yourself.

What was it like to float away so freely? How did the crystal feel in your hands as you drifted?

....

....

....

....

....

....

....

....

....

....

....

TENSION SPOT RELAXATION

If you have been practising relaxation, you will be aware of the areas of your body most prone to knots of tension. These take the longest to relax and are the first to contort if something upsets you.

1. Sit quietly holding your crystal and imagine that it is pulsating with healing energy.

2. When you feel ready, place it on your problem area, imagining it gently radiating calm, emanating a power that dissolves all tension, leaving behind only peace and tranquillity. You can leave your crystal in place for up to 20 minutes, although you may feel benefits much earlier. Cleanse your crystal carefully.

What is your problem area? How does it feel after this ritual?

....
....
....
....
....
....
....

ENTER YOUR CRYSTAL EXERCISE

Prepare for this exercise as you would for scrying (see 'Your Meditation Crystal'). You will need as large a specimen of your crystal as possible – a ball is ideal – so that you can get truly absorbed.

1. Become as relaxed as you can and gaze deep into the centre of your crystal. Focus your eyes on a distant point and imagine that there is a whole world inside your crystal.

2. Imagine your crystal is large, much larger than you thought. It is much bigger than you. In your mind's eye, stand in front of it and admire its wonderful colours, and the subtle shapes you see within it. As you look at it you see that a door is forming. The door has a handle. Grasp the handle, open the door and enter your crystal.

3. At first it seems as if you are in a cave, with crystal walls all around you. You turn, and the door has vanished. You can only wander deeper into the crystal,

meandering through crystalline tunnels, illuminated by a subtle light. Ask for guidance from the crystal spirit and to be shown things that will help you in your quest for relaxation.

4. At this point, the spirit of the crystal will come to guide you. They may take your hand. Now the light within the crystal is growing and the walls around you become smoother until you find yourself in a magnificent hallway, with an atmosphere of welcome, peace and warmth.

5. Along this hallway are many closed doors with handles. You know that in the rooms behind these doors lie important messages for you. Ask your guiding spirit to show you which one to open. Go in and explore the room, noticing all the details.

6. Within these rooms, you may find a wide variety of scenes. Some will contain books, some will show groups of people, some will lead into peaceful gardens. This is a world of peace, tranquillity, enjoyment and blessing. Explore at your leisure and linger as you wish.

7. When the time is right, ask your guardian to lead you back to the original door. Return through the imposing hallway, into the rougher tunnel and find again the door by which you entered, materialized anew for your use. Thank your mentor and bid farewell as you return to the everyday.

This visualization will have shown you messages about what you need in order to relax. Some may not be obvious at first and some might be a surprise. Make no assumptions until you have reflected. Record your observations here.

....
....
....
....
....
....
....
....
....
....
....
....
....
....
....
....
....
....
....
....
....
....

YOUR
HEALING
CRYSTAL

Crystals can be of great help in maintaining the inner harmony and balance that means health. True health is not merely an absence of disease, but a positive state of vitality and pleasure in life. It is important to remember that crystals cannot take the place of professional medical advice.

Few of us are free from 'dis-ease' today. Our lives are stressful and we do not take the time to listen to our bodies or to eat properly. We are bombarded by pollutants of all descriptions, from chemicals in our food to harmful radiation from the technology that surrounds us. 'Dis-ease', or a lack of easefulness and harmony, is at the root of what we know as disease. Not only our bodies, but our souls need healing, since we have cut ourselves off from our true essence, caught in the "head stuff" of modern life. Most of us are vaguely aware that something is amiss, but are unsure exactly what.

Crystals can help redress the balance. Even if you enjoy very good physical health, you can benefit from your own special Healing Crystal to help you feel truly energized. Your Healing Crystal can help when you feel below par, such as when you think you are catching a cold, but it can also be of use when you feel run down and battered by life, when you have simply had a hard and depleting day, or have had to deal with people who drain you. Your Healing Crystal may also be a help if you have a talent for healing others, protecting you as you transfer healing energy.

CHOOSING YOUR HEALING CRYSTAL

Before selecting your crystal it is important to relax and to reflect on your physical, mental and spiritual health. All crystals have healing qualities, but the following have been chosen for their range of attributes. Use the journal spaces provided to write about your health and what wellness means to you, and to record your experiences as you choose this crystal.

YOU WILL NEED

Tumble-stones of the following crystals:
Apache tear, amber, red sardonyx, chrysoprase, blue calcite, turquoise, black tourmaline, rhodonite, smoky quartz, malachite, purple fluorite, moonstone.

Green and blue candles and cloths; lavender oil.

Before you start, take some time to reflect on your current physical, mental and spiritual health. What does health mean to you? Are there ways in which you would like to feel better?

....
....
....
....
....
....
....
....
....
....
....
....

MEDITATION METHOD

This method is based on a feeling of optimum health. If you do not have a specific complaint or simply prefer to concentrate on feeling fantastic, this is the method for you.

Lay out all the crystals before you on a cloth of green or blue | Burn a candle of the same colour if you wish, and to ensure that you relax, place a little lavender oil on your temples or heat it in a burner | Hold your hands in your lap, next to each other, gently cupped | Turn your attention to your body and relax deeply | Now either think about a time in your life when you felt at your peak, bursting with health and vitality; or, if you feel fantastic now, be extra aware of this | Feel the energy gathering in your solar plexus and spreading out, so that your whole body is radiant with it | Hold this feeling for a few moments, then imagine that this feeling is being magnified and prolonged by a crystal held in your cupped hands.

Which of the crystals is it? How strongly does it maginify your feeling of health? Does the feeling seem to be more physical, emotional or mental?

....

....

....

....

....

....

....

....

....

....

COLOUR VISUALIZATION METHOD

You don't need an actual crystal present in order to use this method on a troublesome condition that needs to be healed. The pictures of crystals in this book can be used as a focus.

Simply direct your attention to the part of your body that is troubling you | Give yourself some time for this exercise and be aware that it could evoke difficult feelings if your pain is emotional.

What colour can you visualize soothing it? If you have a pain, what colour would you like to wrap round it?

....
....
....
....
....

Blue or green can calm pain or itching, red or orange can revitalize while black can banish a wart or verruca. Emotional hurts can be healed this way – for instance, disappointment might call for orange or yellow.

Sit quietly, breathe deeply and see what comes into your mind. Go by your instincts. Which stone is the colour that you need?

....
....
....
....
....
....

HEALING MEDITATION METHOD

This is an adaptation of the previous meditation method. Try this if you wish to use your crystal primarily to heal others.

Set out the crystals and settle yourself as before, visualizing a golden glow starting in your solar plexus and radiating outwards | This time, however, be aware that your primary goal is to gather this energy for healing other people, plants or animals | Ask for guidance from whatever higher power or guardian spirit you honour | Imagine that this energy is a gift that you have been given, one that you are going to pass on to others, and visualize this gift emanating from a crystal held in your cupped hands.

Which of the crystals do you see with your mind's eye?
How did you feel when you thought about this crystal
helping you heal others? Focus on the crystal and think
about the words that come to mind.
For example – nurture, love, care.

....
....
....
....
....
....
....
....
....
....
....

INTERPRETING YOUR HEALING CRYSTAL

This section will help you understand your Healing Crystal. The crystal you have chosen may reveal to you areas of your life where you need healing that you had not been aware of. Think about what the crystal is trying to tell you, and journal about how you think it can guide you on your healing journey.

APACHE TEAR

This gentler form of black obsidian coaxes out deeply held emotions and enables the negative to be transformed into the positive. If apache tear is your choice then you may be holding on to old wounds and resentments. This may cause your body to retain toxins and may result in you feeling sluggish and not at your best.

This stone will enable you to understand what is within, to bring it to the light of day, to grieve or rage if you need to; and to let go and move on. Inhibitions can be released and your faith in yourself can be restored. With the comfort of this stone you can achieve understanding and forgiveness, especially of yourself.

Apache tear EASES muscle TENSION, CLEANSES the body and helps vitamin absorption.

....
....
....
....
....
....
....
....
....
....
....
....
....

AMBER

Strictly speaking, amber is not a crystal but fossilized resin from ancient cone-bearing trees, bringing with it the riches of the earth. If you have chosen amber, you may need an injection of optimism. Depression can rob you of your physical vitality, but the heartening influence of this stone stimulates the body and encourages enthusiasm and faith in life.

Amber encourages creativity and clears the mind, so that you can build on a realistic basis to achieve your ambitions. Physically, amber relieves stress by enabling you to see a wider picture and to become balanced and cheerful. It is good for the joints and helps throat and digestive problems. It acts as a tonic for the body's cleansing system by supporting the liver, kidneys and bladder.

Amber REPELS infection and CONNECTS with the ENERGIES of the earth in order to promote healing.

....
....
....
....
....
....
....
....
....
....
....
....
....
....
....

BLUE CALCITE

This stone of peace and trust has a very beneficial effect on the emotions and the nervous system. If you have chosen blue calcite, you may have been through a period of stress and trauma and need peace and rest to recuperate. Blue calcite soothes away anxieties and helps you to be clear about what you feel and why. It enables you to say what you need to say while retaining harmony and tranquillity.

Blue calcite is helpful for any mental work, dissolving blocks to creativity and conferring the strength and positive attitude that can help you overcome obstacles. It is excellent for the bones and skin, helping the immune system and soothing pain and discomfort on all levels.

Blue calcite lowers BLOOD PRESSURE and fosters TRUST in life that will enable you to draw on COSMIC ENERGIES for healing.

....
....
....
....
....
....
....
....
....
....

....

....

....

....

....

....

....

....

....

....

....

....

....

....

....

....

....

....

....

CHRYSOPRASE

This lovely green stone is a wonderful aid to relaxation. If you have been working so hard that you feel you are losing the plot, chrysoprase will enable you to reconnect with the true meaning of life and the beauty of the natural world. Chrysoprase reminds you of your ideals and values and enables you to let go of egotism and judgement in favour of acceptance and love of self and others. In this way it reveals fresh alternatives and encourages a relaxed openness that recognizes opportunities.

It facilitates a good night's sleep, free of nightmares, and calms phobias. If you wish to conceive, this stone can boost fertility and generally enhance the health of the sexual organs, bringing fulfilment.

Chrysoprase REGULATES the HORMONES and helps the body to EXPEL toxins.

....

....

BLACK TOURMALINE

This is a stone for strength and defence. If you have chosen black tourmaline, you may feel you are under threat or have many challenges to meet for which you will need all your resources. Black tourmaline has the power to repel attack on a psychic level and to give you the physical vitality to do whatever needs to be done on the practical side. Best of all, it enables you to keep your cool, so everything is kept in proportion and manageable.

One of this stone's most valuable uses is to protect against electromagnetic energies from computers and mobiles – for this purpose it can be worn around the neck.

Black tourmaline draws negative energy away from the body, BALANCES the brain hemispheres, helps ARTHRITIS and is beneficial for the SPINE.

::

::

::

::

::

::

::

::

::

::

::

::

::

organize your mind and environment, enabling you to scrutinize your habits and subconscious motivations and to change them if necessary.

This stone enables you to access your intuition and develop psychic gifts while retaining common sense. It will help you to heal yourself through meditation.

Fluorite is also good for INFLAMMATION, colds and NERVE PAIN and is a TONIC for sexual desires, especially if these have been dampened by disillusionment.

::

::

::

::

::

::

::

::

::

::

::

PURPLE FLUORITE

A very spiritual stone, purple fluorite encourages psychic fine tuning. If you have chosen purple fluorite you may fear that you are being manipulated and invaded on a subtle level and realize that you need to shut down and protect yourself while attuning to higher states of consciousness. However, it also helps you

MALACHITE

This powerful stone needs to be used with care, so if you have chosen malachite take time to attune deeply to your intuitive reactions and limit contact with the stone until you are sure it is benefiting you. Malachite is very good at releasing negativity; if you have picked it you may badly need to cleanse yourself of something unpleasant or destructive, and to have the courage to move forward into a totally new space. You can't kid yourself or others while under the influence of malachite and, as a result, outworn ties may be broken as strong emotions surface.

However, it is also a stone of profound empathy. Malachite heals all sexual problems (including traumas from childhood) and helps with problems including menstruation and childbirth.

Malachite treats GROWTHS, REPELS TOXINS and is good for TRAVEL SICKNESS.

....
....
....
....
....
....
....
....
....
....
....
....
....

....
....

MOONSTONE

This stone makes you aware of your dreams as the language of your subconscious. By getting to know yourself at a deep level you can make a new start in life. If you have chosen moonstone you may feel alienated from yourself and have lost contact with that "still small voice" within.

Moonstone brings body wisdom, aligning the instincts with the intellect. It is a very feminine stone and can help women contact the Goddess within, or help men to find their feminine side. It encourages you to "go with the flow" and draws out and heals the emotions, soothes the digestion and stabilizes hormones.

It helps with SHOCK and disorders such as ADHD (attention deficit hyperactivity disorder), and is particularly good for the FEMININE reproductive system.

....
....
....
....
....
....
....

....
....
....
....
....
....
....
....

RED SARDONYX

An excellent energy source, red sardonyx provides stimulation and encouragement in all areas of life. If you have chosen red sardonyx, you may need an infusion of élan to make a fresh assault on life, to get out of a rut, achieve a cherished ambition and to strengthen your willpower. Red sardonyx will give you vitality but it will also help you to exercise control and draw on your deepest wells of stamina.

It is a stone of decision and determination, attracting good fortune through a positive attitude. This stone also confers protection by helping you to be true to yourself. It helps you attract partners that complement you and bring you joy. It sharpens all the senses.

Red sardonyx is a STIMULANT to the metabolism, also helping the LUNGS and IMMUNE system.

....
....
....
....
....
....
....
....
....
....
....

TURQUOISE

Lovely turquoise helps you to see how beautiful life is even at its simplest, and encourages you to count your blessings. If you have chosen turquoise you may have become self-pitying and have turned into your own worst enemy. This stone will enable you to be calm and positive, and to find things that bring you joy and release creativity.

Turquoise alleviates panic attacks and fears of speaking in public and protects against pollution from the environment. It is a friend in times of exhaustion or depletion from environmental causes.

Because it confers serenity it creates the right state of mind for making romantic contacts and for having fun. Laughter – a great tonic to the immune system – is more readily provoked with this stone.

Physically, turquoise SOOTHES inflammation, STIMULATES the absorption of nutrients and FIGHTS infection.

....

....

....

....

....

....

....

....

....

....

....

....

....

....

....

SMOKY QUARTZ

This stone forms a powerful connection to the earth and so aids in grounding and stabilizing. It is important to be sure the stone is natural, not irradiated. If you have chosen smoky quartz you may feel you are going through a period of unavoidable difficulty and need a steady stream of supportive energy to help you through. Smoky quartz will calm your fears and help you to take each day as it comes, finding comfort and enjoyment in day-to-day things.

It helps concentration and practicality, and in the end will guide you towards the realization of your dreams. Physically it helps increase tolerance levels, eases headaches, generally stimulates, strengthens and encourages the body to absorb minerals.

Smoky quartz is good for the REPRODUCTIVE organs, MUSCLES, nerves and HEART.

....

....

....

....

....

....

....

....

....

....

....

....

RHODONITE

This stone of warmth and harmony carries the message that love is the greatest healing force of all. If you have chosen rhodonite you may feel you have suffered through coldness – either your own or the coldness of others – and that you want to be able to open out, to give, to make contact and be positive.

Rhodonite can connect you to the healing and nurturing powers of a community, enabling you to take without guilt and give without counting the cost. It heals abuse and destructive relationship patterns, encourages the release of emotions, responsibility and true forgiveness. Best of all, it promotes healthy self-love that enables you to truly love others. It is excellent for trauma and extreme emotional states.

Rhodonite is good for the HEARING, for healing WOUNDS and bites, and for boosting FERTILITY.

....
....
....
....
....
....
....

HEALING
RITUALS

The following pages contain rituals, meditations and
visualizations for you to practise.

Working with your Healing Crystal can help you identify
areas in your life and body in which you need healing, and
can guide you toward wellness. It can also lead you to a
better understanding of what health is to you.

Use the journal spaces to record your experiences of these
rituals, and to keep track of your overall health as you work
through them.

SOUL HEALING MEDITATION

Wounds to the soul can occur in childhood due to trauma or abuse, or can be from a past life. These wounds interfere with growth and stop us having the harmonious relationship with the world that is our birthright. Soul healing may be a deep matter, but with the aid of your crystal it is possible to make a start.

1. Make sure your surroundings feel safe and that you will not be disturbed. Cover yourself with a green shawl (or any colour that feels right) and lie down holding your crystal over your heart.

2. Try to relax and ask to be taken back in time to when the trauma occurred. Do not worry if this image does not come to you clearly. You can simply imagine yourself as a small child who is hurt, or a wounded adult if your intuition suggests past-life involvement. When you have this image in your mind, send love and compassion to this person and imagine your crystal growing larger and larger, wrapping itself around the hurt person like a glowing bubble. Within this chamber of love and peace, the wounds are being healed; see the person becoming whole and happy.

3. You may need to do this a number of times before you feel it is complete. After each session, give thanks, cleanse your crystal and take a drink of spring water.

What time or image did you visualize to try and connect with the wounds to your soul? How did it feel to imagine these wounds being soothed and healed by the crystal?

....
....
....
....
....
....
....
....
....
....
....
....
....
....

HEALING OTHERS RITUAL

Many people – perhaps all of us – are able to transfer healing energies to those who need them. Crystals can certainly help. All healing should only be done with the consent and co-operation of the person being healed, otherwise it is an infringement of boundaries – or even an ego-trip.

1. Try to obtain a clear quartz wand – natural or shaped – to use in addition to your Healing Crystal, but if this is not possible, use your fingers to direct the energy instead. Whenever you are healing, ask for guidance from the higher power or force you believe in and to be aware that the energy you are channelling is not the property of your own ego but comes from the cosmos.

2. Face the person and hold your Healing Crystal close to your abdomen with your passive hand. Affirm that you are drawing energy within you. Feel it flowing up through your legs from the earth, and gathering in your solar plexus. Feel light drawing down from above through the crown of your head, meeting the other energy source within you. Feel your crystal amplifying this energy and be aware of it as a golden glow.

3. Hold your quartz wand in your active hand, direct this energy into your arm and down into the wand. Point the wand at the part of the body to be healed and imagine a stream of light entering it from the wand, healing all hurts. When you have finished, consciously close yourself

off from external energy, eat and drink something, and cleanse both your crystal and the quartz wand.

Record your experiences of this ritual here. How did it feel to perform healing on someone else? What did they tell you about their experience of the ritual?

....
....
....
....
....
....
....
....
....
....
....
....
....

PHYSICAL HEALING RITUALS

Your Healing Crystal can help with any bodily problem; the simplest way is by direct contact with the skin. Here are a few different ways you can use your crystal in physical healing rituals.

* If you have pain in any part of your body, place the crystal as close to the pain as you can. Visualize the colour of the crystal bathing the area, taking away all the discomfort. Hold this image for as long as you can, and you should gain significant relief.

* Lie comfortably with your crystal close by. Imagine the spirit of the crystal emerging from within, growing to human size and standing beside you. Now imagine this spirit ministering to you. You may ask for advice if you wish, and you may "hear" the answer within your mind. When the time feels right, thank your crystal spirit before you say goodbye.

* Place your crystal in pure spring water for an hour or so, so that the water may absorb some of the crystal's energies. Dab the energized water on any affected areas of your body.

Which of these rituals seems to work best for you? Why do you think that is? What kind of pain are you trying to heal?

....
....
....
....
....
....
....
....
....
....
....
....
....
....
....
....
....

YOUR PROTECTION CRYSTAL

Most crystals have protective qualities because their calming and balancing influence has a beneficial effect on the environment. However, your Protection Crystal is intended to do more than that, and can strengthen your inner and outer defences by adding its energy to yours.

Occultists and clairvoyants tell us that we all have an aura – a sheath of energy surrounding the body that appears in many different colours and layers. A clairvoyant may be able to discern characteristics such as strength and spirituality in the aura. Although you may not realize it, a strong and vibrant aura can offer you protection against many things, because it is sensed at a subconscious level by those who might cause harm, and also because it repels negative energies generally while attracting positive ones. With its sympathetic vibrations, your Protection Crystal can help to strengthen your aura.

Often the most obvious threats are the easiest to deal with, while the subtle ones may be more insidious. For instance, it can be difficult to identify and confront a person who is leeching your energy or undermining you. Your Protection Crystal can deal with the problem where it starts – at the energy level. However, it is important that you also take practical action to keep yourself safe. For instance, while garnet protects against attack, your best defence is to keep away from dangerous neighbourhoods. One of the most valuable gifts offered by your Protection Crystal is that it strengthens your intuitions about safety.

Once you have chosen your Protection Crystal, try to obtain two or more pieces of your crystal – one to wear, one for work, one for home and so on. Wearing your crystal is good all-round protection, but having a large crystal where you can see it is a great additional boost.

CHOOSING YOUR
PROTECTION CRYSTAL

The following crystals have been selected for their variety of protective qualities, but each one can have the effect of strengthening your own protective abilities and instincts in all areas. Use the journal spaces to record your feelings as you go through this process. Think about what protection means to you, and what makes you feel safe.

YOU WILL NEED

Choose from:
malachite, labradorite, bloodstone, snowflake obsidian, garnet, chalcedony, lapis lazuli, jet, onyx, jade, carnelian and red jasper.

Dark-coloured ribbon, candle; lavender oil and joss stick.

What does safety feel like to you? What kind of situations or places make you feel less safe and secure? What would you like to change about this?

....
....
....
....
....
....
....
....
....
....
....
....
....
....

THE CLOTH BAG METHOD

Just as you did with the Personality Crystal, simply place the crystals or their substitutes in a cloth bag | Close your eyes, become calm and state clearly from what you want to be protected | Ask for guidance, reach into the bag and take your pick.

How did you feel as you reached into the bag? Nervous? Vulnerable? Brave? Which crystal did you choose, and what kind of protection do you feel it can give you? Does it make you feel safer, or stronger, or more aware of what you can do to keep yourself safe?

....

....

....

....

....

....

....

THE VISUALIZATION METHOD

This method is an expansion of the above, but will give you the opportunity to tune in to the spirits of the crystals. You may like to prepare for it with a cleansing bath in which you have sprinkled a little lavender essential oil. Play relaxing music to get you in the mood and burn a pleasant joss stick.

Make sure you won't be disturbed | For this method, it is truly necessary to have each of the crystals, at least in the form of tumble-stones, set out before you | Prepare for the exercise in the same way as the circle method, but before imagining your fear, visualize a spirit rising out of each crystal | If your powers of visualization are good, you may see them forming quite clearly and you may feel you can communicate with them | One may seem especially powerful and sympathetic and you may feel drawn to this one | If you do not feel clear, visualize your fear as described in the Circle Method below | Now observe which of the crystal spirits goes forth to do battle with and destroy your fear.

Did you feel drawn to one crystal immediately, or did you need to visualize your fear before your Protection Crystal became apparent? Which crystal did you choose? How does the crystal make you feel?

....

....

....

....

....

....

....

....

....

THE CIRCLE METHOD

Arrange the ribbon in a circle on the floor with the crystals (or representations) in a line, roughly towards the north of your circle (or south if you live in the southern hemisphere) | Light a candle to stand behind the crystals and place yourself inside your circle of safety | Take with you something that makes you feel safe, such as a picture of a friend, or even a teddy bear you loved as a child | Affirm that you are safe, close your eyes and become calm and steady | Visualize your fear materializing behind the candle | Even if it is something formless, like depression, give it a shape if you can, or failing that a sound, smell or sensation | Now ask yourself which crystal is going to zap that fear | Visualize a white laser-beam striking the fear and destroying it | The crystal that produces the white beam is your Protection Crystal.

What was the fear you chose to visualize? How did you visualize it? What was this ritual like for you? How did it feel when you visualized your Protection Crystal producing the white beam?

....

....

....

....

....

....

....

....

....

....

....

....

....

....

IF YOUR CHOICE DOES NOT FIT

Maybe you were worried about your child, yet your choice has been carnelian; or your career concerns you, yet jet has come forward. Trust your crystal – while it may seem as if you are doing the choosing, the truth may be the reverse. So use the crystal that has "picked" you, adapting to suit; place carnelian near your child's bed as well as your own, place jet on your desk as well as over your hearth. Improvise and combine them until you feel sure of where the true need lies.

INTERPRETING YOUR PROTECTION CRYSTAL

These pages offer interpretations of the various Protection Crystals. Do you identify with the description of your crystal? Does it make sense when you consider the things you would like to feel protected from?

BLOODSTONE

Since ancient Babylonian times, bloodstone has been credited with the ability to repel enemies. Soldiers carried it to prevent wounds and halt bleeding, and even today it may be used to stop nosebleeds, no doubt simply through the coolness and pressure of the stone. If this is your choice then you may fear literal cuts, threats to your physical vigour, or you may have to undergo an operation.

Bloodstone keeps anything harmful at bay and strengthens your own ability to avoid danger by using your wits and common sense. Wearing bloodstone protects your health. Hold it below the waist, for strength.

Bloodstone keeps you CONNECTED to the here and now, so that you can be FOCUSED and EFFECTIVE.

....

....

....

....

....

....

....

....

....

....

....

....

....

....

....

....

....

....

....

....

CARNELIAN

This is a wonderful stone for courage, protecting generally from negativity and the harmful influences of the past. It is especially good for public speaking, something that is increasingly required professionally and of which many people are afraid. Carnelian was also believed to guard against others knowing your thoughts or against "enchantments".

Carnelian guards the home against storms, keeps anger and spite at bay, and it drives away the fear of death. If you have chosen this stone then you are aware that you need a major dose of strength, confidence and vitality, but also to feel peacefully aligned to the cycles of life.

Wear carnelian as a pendant for a source of ENCOURAGEMENT and to show that you are a FORCE to be RECKONED with.

....
....
....
....
....
....
....
....
....
....

GARNET

This is a very strong stone, bringing with it powers of endurance and great energy. If you have chosen this stone, you may be facing a particular challenge, either physical or mental. Garnet will protect and conserve your energy levels. In times gone by it was thought to drive away demons and to warn the wearer of approaching danger.

Garnet will strengthen your auric sheath and if you visualize this, your "vibes" may discourage a would-be attacker. Traditionally garnet offers protection against thieves and it is also beneficial for health. If you feel "there is no way out" garnet will help you find one and turn you into a survivor. Wear as earrings to sense any approaching threat.

Wear garnet as CLOSE to your HEART as you can to feel EMPOWERED.

....
....
....
....

....

....

....

....

....

....

....

....

....

....

....

....

instability – chalcedony can bring you encouragement, faith in yourself and feelings of *joie de vivre*. This stone also offers protection in lawsuits.

Wear chalcedony as a RING or necklace to feel cared for and SAFE in the WORLD.

....

....

....

....

....

....

....

....

....

....

....

....

....

CHALCEDONY

This stone protects against bad dreams and negative thinking. It also dispels illusions of all kinds and alleviates sadness. If you have "the jitters" it can calm you and may also be effective for more extreme types of mental disturbance. It has long been considered a protective talisman for travellers, preventing accidents and mishaps, and it protects the home and the family.

If you have chosen this stone, you may be deceived by a person or situation – or deceiving yourself. At an instinctive level you realize this and have come to chalcedony to dispel this. Or it may be that you are moving around a lot and face

JADE

Jade has many protective qualities. It is especially good for protecting the body from disease, and will also protect your plants if four pieces are placed around the edges of your garden, roughly at the compass points. Because it brings wisdom it averts bad judgement and stops you being manipulated. In the same way, it helps to prevent accidents.

The Chinese believe that jade prolongs life, and they eat from jade bowls to absorb the benefits of the stone. If you have chosen jade, you may sense your best protection is to tune in to the benefits of Nature, to seek peace, care for your body and go with the flow. Jade heals the kidneys and bladder and may be worn on the belt, or anywhere next to the skin for maximum effect.

Jade brings HARMONY and helps to ATTRACT FRIENDS.

....
....
....
....
....
....
....
....
....
....
....
....
....
....
....
....
....
....

RED JASPER

Jasper works on many levels to keep you safe. It protects you from your own desires, which could lead to danger. In ancient times jasper was believed to protect against poisoning and to guard mother and child during childbirth. It repels all negativity, sending it back to the source. If you have chosen this stone, you may feel you need to get a handle on things. Face conflict if you have to and be honest with yourself.

Jasper helps to keep you grounded and to nurture yourself in tough times. Best of all, it helps you put your finger on what is wrong before it gets out of proportion, and it enables justice to be done. Place it close to the base of your spine to feel detoxified or wear as jewellery.

Red jasper is a stone of HEALTH, strength and VITALITY, increasing BEAUTY and attractiveness.

....
....
....
....
....
....
....
....

....
....
....
....
....
....

JET

Jet is not really a crystal, but fossilized wood. It has been used for protection since the Stone Age. Placed on a newborn baby's stomach, it guards the child. Worn as an amulet, it protects the traveller in unfamiliar surroundings. Jet is also a protection when embarking on inner journeys such as visualizations, and it guards the health.

If you have chosen jet, you may possess deep knowledge from many incarnations, and realize that your best protection is experience and the wisdom of the planet Earth. Jet is a very receptive stone and is believed to merge with the body of the owner, so pre-owned jet should be cleansed assiduously. Wear jet as a necklace to take control.

Jet REPELS nightmares and all SPIRITS of EVIL and DARKNESS.

....
....

....
....
....
....
....
....
....
....
....
....
....
....
....
....
....
....
....
....

LABRADORITE

This stone of psychic protection will strengthen the aura and preserve its energies. It will guard you particularly from the thoughts of other people, especially their unconscious expectations and beliefs about you. Labradorite will make it impossible for these to attach to you and subvert you. If you have chosen labradorite, you may recognize that your main purpose is a spiritual one and you wish to hold on to this and avoid contamination.

Labradorite will also help you resist base impulses and distractions. It repels all negativity, including your own as you become aware of it. It can be worn as a necklace over the heart or held for inspiration and to balance the bodily processes.

Labradorite stone will be a SUPPORTIVE COMPANION through CHANGE.

....
....
....
....
....
....
....
....
....
....
....
....
....
....

LAPIS LAZULI

In ancient Sumer this stone was closely associated with deities, so wearing it invoked the protection of the gods. It is also associated with the great Egyptian goddess Isis. It protects the bond between lovers. In modern day India it is used to protect children who wear it as a necklace to keep them healthy and to help them grow.

If you have chosen lapis lazuli you may be especially aware of the need for loving, caring and nurturing thoughts, both from yourself and those around you, to protect the interests of those you love. It enables you to remain calm and able to say the right thing at the right time to promote your best interests. It is best worn at the throat.

This stone REPELS SUFFERING and CRUELTY.

....
....
....
....
....
....
....
....
....
....
....
....
....
....

MALACHITE

This stone is believed to warn the owner of impending danger. According to legend, malachite will break in pieces as a sign that danger is approaching. It protects financial affairs, especially if placed at the four corners of an office or building.

A very powerful stone, malachite needs to be used with care as it magnifies all energies, including negative energies. It absorbs pollution.

Mostly, however, malachite protects from stagnation, so if you have chosen it you want to preserve your ability to transform and move on, even if this might be uncomfortable at times.

Use only polished malachite. Place it on your navel to recover from old traumas or wear as preferred.

NOTE: Remove malachite at once if you experience palpitations.

Generally, malachite GUARDS against NEGATIVITY and physical DANGER, especially danger from falling.

....
....
....
....
....
....

ONYX

Onyx protects against enemies of all kinds. If onyx is your choice you may feel vulnerable and want to keep your head down and shut off in general. It is possible you are afraid of exposing yourself or letting yourself down.

This stone will keep your secrets. Onyx will give you stamina and the strength to look beyond present challenging circumstances into a more promising future. Wear onyx on your left hand (if right-handed) to harmonize with the restrained character of the stone.

Onyx is GROUNDING and SUPPORTING, a stone to lean on and to learn from when gaining CONTROL of your life.

....
....
....

....
....
....
....
....
....
....
....
....
....
....
....
....

SNOWFLAKE OBSIDIAN

All forms of obsidian are highly protective for they block and mop up negative energy. Snowflake obsidian is a gentler form of the stone, and is less likely to demand self-analysis from you. If you have chosen this stone, you may be afraid of fear itself, frightened by your own negative thinking. Or you may be truly under attack on a spiritual level from someone who is sending ill wishes your way; only by fearing this can you let it through your defences.

Snowflake obsidian will strengthen your faith in yourself and enable you to feel solidly in contact with Mother Earth. Hold snowflake obsidian against you, very low down on your abdomen, to give you "guts" and imagine it forming a dark, protective cloak around you.

This stone is PROTECTIVE and is able to ABSORB NEGATIVE energy.

....
....
....
....
....
....
....
....
....
....
....
....
....
....
....
....
....

PROTECTION RITUALS

The following pages contain rituals, meditations and
visualizations for you to practise.

Working with your Protection Crystal can help you feel
empowered in situations where you might feel unsafe or
vulnerable, and it can help you identify areas in your life
where you were feeling uncomfortable or unsafe without
necessarily realizing.

Use the journal spaces to record your experiences of
these practices.

CRYSTAL SPIRIT DEFENCE VISUALIZATION

If you are coping with a threatening situation or person at home or at work, this visualization will boost your ability to look after yourself and ensure that you have a powerful ally on the subtle planes brought by your crystal.

1. This is an expansion of the visualization method for choosing your crystal (see pages 71–72), and may be prepared for in a similar way, by bathing and playing music. A patchouli joss stick is a good choice, but lavender, frankincense, pine and rose are also linked with protection and will help you to "tune in".

2. Place your crystal in front of you, surrounded by four candles set in a protective square to symbolize the four directions. A large piece of crystal – a pyramid, wand, cluster or ball – would be good here. Relax and watch the reflections of the candles in the crystal.

3. Now visualize an angel rising out of the crystal. See it take shape, growing to life-size, becoming brighter and more detailed. Try to see your angel's face; speak with it, if you can. Ask your angel to be with you and protect you. See that your angel has a sword or other weapon that shatters deceit and repels all spite, attack and negativity.

4. This weapon is effective against negativity – it does no harm to anyone although anyone malevolent will be repelled. Ask your angel to stand behind or beside you and to remain with you. It will stay with you, but may gradually fade, so boost its strength by drawing on your crystal again, with this exercise, as necessary.

How did you feel when you saw the angel? What did the angel look like to you?

....
....
....
....
....
....
....
....
....

SELF PROTECTION RITUAL

This exercise strengthens your auric sheath, so that you will be safe from harm. It draws on the powers of the Earth and your own special crystal, to create "generators" to boost your aura.

You will need a joss stick of patchouli, lavender, pine, frankincense or rose; a wine glass filled with spring water; an orange or gold candle; 6 metres (20 ft) of string or ribbon in any dark colour that symbolizes safety for you. You may take with you an object or charm that makes you feel safe.

1. Many of us feel threatened, and this can be a barrier to progress and happiness; this exercise is of great benefit, so set aside a few peaceful hours to give it your full attention. Go for a walk in the country or parkland and find a sizeable flat stone, perhaps 12 cm (5 in) square – take your time with this. Cleanse this in a stream or soak it in spring water for an hour.

2. When you return home, have a relaxing bath containing a few drops of lavender oil. Arrange your area with the lit candle in the south symbolizing fire, the stone in the north (for earth), the joss stick in the east (for air) and the wine glass in the west (for water). These are associations that have been used by occultists for centuries. If you live in the southern hemisphere, reverse earth and fire, since the sun is in your north. Place your string or ribbon in a circle around your body, and have your stone and Protection Crystal ready.

3. Start by facing your stone and say: "May the powers of earth enter this crystal, protecting from all physical harm." Imagine physical strength and barriers, affirming that your crystal holds this. Now turn to the east, saying: "May the powers of air enter this crystal, protecting from mental harm and harsh words." Imagine bright, pure thought and an ability to "rise above" entering your crystal. Face the candle and say: "May the powers of fire enter this crystal, giving spiritual protection, courage and energy." Imagine your crystal vibrant with inner fire. Face the wine glass, saying: "May the powers of water enter this crystal, protecting the heart and emotions, and healing."

Imagine your crystal holds soothing waters or amniotic fluid as in the womb.

4. Turn back to the stone and place your crystal on top of it. Visualize an energy-beam coming from this now formidable crystal, strengthening your aura until it is intense, strong and impermeable.

5. To finish, extinguish the candle, pour the water from the glass out on to the earth and bind the string around the stone. Keep this safe, to use again.

Affirm that you are back in the here and now by patting your body all over. Store your crystal as appropriate. Whenever you need an extra burst of protective power, look at your crystal and imagine that energy-beam coming towards you again. You are protected on all sides and in all ways.

This is a long ritual – what was the process like for you? Write about your experiences of finding the stone and setting up your space. How do you feel now that your crystal is suffused with this protective energy?

....

....

....

....

....

....

....

....

....

....

....

....

....

....

....

YOUR
MEDITATION
CRYSTAL

Meditation is an altered state of consciousness in
which your mind has access to inspiration and insight,
or a means to experience a oneness with the world that
is very healing and uplifting.

There is nothing strange about this state of mind, since we approach it whenever we daydream, although we may fail to realize its power. Meditation also includes visualization and inner journeys. All such practices are helpful in today's hectic and materialistic environment.

The crystal you choose for meditation will enable you to leave this world behind and to enter a peaceful alternative reality that some call the astral plane. Occultists believe that on this plane the imagination is very powerful, and that things you wish to create first take shape there, before being translated to ordinary reality. Your crystal can help you focus your true wishes clearly and effectively, by aiding your ability to visualize.

However, please do not worry if you find it hard to visualize, for it is possible to gain the benefits of meditation in peace and stillness.

CHOOSING YOUR MEDITATION CRYSTAL

Choosing your Meditation Crystal is a "meditation" in itself. Find a quiet place where you won't be disturbed and set aside time to determine which of the crystals will aid your meditation practice. Use the journal spaces to record your experiences as you select your crystal.

YOU WILL NEED

Choose from:
amethyst, ametrine, clear quartz, black obsidian, chrysocolla, golden beryl, celestite, sodalite, rhodochrosite, green agate, selenite and azurite.

Purple or violet candle.

Before you begin, what do you hope your Meditation Crystal will help you achieve? Would you like your meditation to become more focused? Do you want it to leave you feeling tranquil or energized?

....
....
....
....
....
....
....
....
....
....
....
....

THE VISUALIZATION METHOD

Make certain that you will not be disturbed while you meditate | Burn a purple or violet candle and place your tumble-stones, or their representations, around it | Sit or lie down comfortably | Relax and become aware of your breathing | In your mind, go to a place in the real, natural world that you love and with which you have a special affinity – this may be a woodland clearing, a lakeside spot, a rocky beach or whatever comes to your mind | Take as long as you like to imagine this | Be aware of an entrance to a cave in your peaceful place | Go towards it | Deep within the cave is a light, similar to that of your candle, only much brighter | Around it are grouped the spirits of the crystals in a shimmering cluster, radiant with divine blessings | Ask the spirit of your crystal to come to you, to guide you | Wait patiently | The spirit that comes to take your hand is your guide on inner journeys, and the crystal they come from is your Meditation Crystal | You may now journey further with your crystal spirit or give thanks and come back to everyday awareness.

What place did you visualize for this meditation? Describe it here. What was it like waiting for the crystal spirit to step forward? How did you feel when the spirit took your hand?

....
....
....
....
....
....
....
....
....

THE CHAKRAS

The chakras are important to meditation. These are organs or centres in the spiritual body – the body that has its existence in the astral plane, but which occupies the same space as your physical body. Some people are able to leave their physical body and travel consciously in the astral plane, while we all do this nightly in our dreams. Deep meditative states have some elements in common with astral travel.

As you meditate, it is likely that your chakras – essentially energy centres – will be activated. Certain crystals have an affinity with specific chakras. There are seven main chakras to consider. These are situated on the crown, the brow, the throat, the chest, the solar plexus, the lower abdomen and the base of the spine.

CROWN

THIRD EYE

THROAT

HEART

SOLAR PLEXUS

SACRAL

BASE

Starting with the base chakra and the colour red, they correspond, in order, with the seven colours of the rainbow. Crystals are often linked to a chakra because of colour correspondence. Full instruction on opening the chakras is outside the scope of this book, but when you use your crystal, you may be aware of one or all of your chakras opening. It is very important that you close them after each exercise, or you could feel depleted and open to unpleasant influences, either from disturbing humans or spirit entities.

Do this by imagining them shutting tightly like flower petals reverting to bud and by affirming strongly that you are closing down, and/or by eating and drinking.

The Base Chakra relates to survival and the organs of elimination (and sexuality to some extent). The Sacral Chakra relates to the sexual organs and is about intimacy and deep feelings. The Solar Plexus Chakra relates to the central nervous system and digestion, also to the sense of self, development and creativity.

The Heart Chakra is naturally related to the heart as an organ and to all it connects with, and spiritually to the capacity to love, empathize and feel compassion. The Throat Chakra is concerned with the speech centres and the ability to communicate. The Brow Chakra is the "Third Eye", relating to the brain and more subtle perceptions. Finally, the Crown Chakra is our link with the Divine and with true enlightenment.

Try meditating with your crystal and see if you have an awareness of any of your chakras opening. What does this feel like? Does the crystal make this sense stronger? Think about the different chakras and what they mean to you.

....
....
....
....
....
....
....
....
....
....
....
....

INTERPRETING YOUR MEDITATION CRYSTAL

These pages explore the different Meditation Crystals and how each one can be interpreted. Read the description of your crystal and see if it resonates with you. Use the space provided to journal about why you think you were drawn to this crystal (or why this crystal chose you).

AMETHYST

This wonderful purple stone is extremely spiritual and protective. If you have chosen this stone, you may already be attuned to higher states of consciousness, or have a deep desire to be so. Amethyst links with the Third Eye Chakra, and if you place it on this part of your body it can open your perceptions. It connects you, gently and completely, to the realms of spirit and the inspirations of the astral plane.

Meditating with amethyst facilitates astral travel and sleeping with it under your pillow will bring revealing, yet peaceful dreams. Your choice of amethyst shows deep understanding, a profound tranquillity but also the sense of adventure to explore the subtle realms.

This stone confers wisdom, but also acts as a GUARDIAN against INVASION on the spiritual planes, TRANSMUTING negativity into love.

....
....
....
....
....
....
....
....
....
....
....
....

AMETRINE

This crystal is a combination of amethyst and citrine, formed as heat within the Earth was transforming amethyst into citrine. It brings with it the spiritual gifts of amethyst, plus the mental clarity of citrine. If you have chosen this stone, you may want to be able to make intellectual sense of your insights and to be able to use them creatively in the earthly realm.

Place ametrine on your solar plexus to coax deep issues to the surface, enabling you to express them clearly, freeing yourself to explore and create without excess baggage. Meditating with ametrine enables you to embrace paradox and unite the masculine and feminine sides of your nature.

Your choice of ametrine shows DYNAMISM and a wish to control your own life, drawing on WELLSPRINGS of wisdom and UNIVERSAL love.

....
....
....
....
....
....
....
....
....
....
....
....
....
....
....

GOLDEN BERYL

This is called the stone of the seer and was the original "crystal ball". The crystal of the Elizabethan occultist Dr John Dee, now housed in the British Museum, is made of beryl. It is a wonderful stone for scrying (page 101). It is associated with the Crown and Solar Plexus Chakras. If you have chosen beryl, you may long for a less stressful life where you can leave behind the tedious and unimportant and concentrate on spirituality and fundamental priorities.

Placed on the solar plexus, beryl enables you to relax completely; placed on the top of the head, it encourages total focus and may bring strong insights. Choosing beryl indicates that you want to sort out your priorities and manifest what is really important in your life.

Beryl allows you to start sorting out your priorities. This starts with effective and very clear use of the IMAGINATION to CREATE on the ASTRAL plane.

....
....
....
....
....
....

....
....
....
....
....
....
....
....
....

....
....
....
....
....
....
....
....
....
....
....
....
....
....

AZURITE

This stone facilitates astral travel and may help in channelling. This is a process where an individual may deliver messages from the subtle realms. If you decide that you have the ability to channel, you will find you are saying things almost without the intervention of your conscious mind. Your choice of azurite indicates that you wish to communicate on a higher level, although this may not take the form of literal channelling, but may mean you want to convey your spirituality to others.

Azurite helps you let go of old, outworn beliefs, especially fears and phobias, which it helps you to understand and transmute. Help for this may be received during meditation, with azurite on the throat or Third Eye (see page 103).

Choosing azurite shows that you SEEK a NEW REALITY.

GREEN AGATE

Agate has a strong connection to the natural world and the Earth. If you have chosen green agate, you may be powerfully aware of the divine in Nature and are able to enter mystical states through contact with plants and trees, or you may sense that you could develop this.

If you meditate with green agate on your Heart Chakra, it can open you to a profound love and compassion for all that lives on the Earth, and in turn you will feel nourished. This stone stabilizes and balances. If you have been emotionally traumatized it will enable you to see the bigger picture, to be soothed and to move on in life.

If you have chosen green agate you are DECISIVE (or would like to be) and able to find PRACTICAL SOLUTIONS to problems.

....
....
....
....
....
....
....
....
....
....
....
....
....
....
....
....

CHRYSOCOLLA

This tranquil stone enables you to find and maintain inner peace when all around

you is in a state of flux. If you have chosen this stone, you may wish to stay in contact with the spiritual essence within you to help you cope with insecurity and instability. Or you may be blessed with the knowledge that change brings opportunity and you are able to go with the flow.

Chrysocolla may be placed at the Heart Chakra to heal sorrow and enable love to flow anew. At the Throat Chakra it facilitates calm, clear communication and confers the wisdom to know when silence would be best. If you have been feeling burdened by guilt, meditating with chrysocolla on your heart will enable you to forgive yourself.

Choosing chrysocolla SHOWS STABILITY and SERENITY.

....
....
....
....
....
....
....
....
....
....
....
....

CLEAR QUARTZ

This crystal holds the key to the widest possible range of knowledge and wisdom. If you have chosen clear quartz you are a seeker after truth and may want the answer to fundamental questions. Quartz can increase your energy, both physical and spiritual, and may be placed on any of the chakras for corresponding benefit. It also has the gift of harmonizing the chakras, regulating the energy flow in your subtle body, making you alert, yet tranquil and very clear in mind, emotions and spirit.

Clear quartz can release buried memories, both from this life and former lives, and helps you to develop your psychic abilities and awareness.

If you have chosen clear quartz you have psychic energy that you wish to focus, but you need to be FREE of DISTRACTIONS and achieve BALANCE.

....

....

....

....

....

....

....

....

....

....

....

....

....

....

....

....

CELESTITE

This New Age stone is similar to angelite. Avoid leaving it in sunlight or its delicate colour will fade. Celestite is a great boost towards spiritual development. If you have chosen this stone, you may feel that you want a push to enable you to begin exploring new forms of spirituality. Celestite will lead you to fortunate contacts that will help you on your path. It facilitates dream recall and astral travel, but it also brings peace and strength.

Celestite is especially helpful when placed on the Third Eye Chakra where it tunes you in to Universal wisdom. Choice of celestite may mean that you need to leave mundane worries behind. It helps you to combine your intuition with your intellect to feel sure of your path and to communicate this clearly and peacefully.

Celestite placed anywhere in the room will RAISE vibrations and is GOOD for GROUP meditation.

You may also be aware of angelic messengers and wish to encourage them. Selenite resonates with the Crown Chakra and is deeply spiritual, so if you have chosen it you may wish to develop this side of yourself.

Selenite also helps TELEPATHIC CONTACT, especially if each person involved HOLDS a piece of selenite.

....

....

....

....

....

....

....

....

....

....

....

....

....

....

....

....

....

....

....

....

....

....

....

....

....

....

....

SELENITE

This stone has a very fine vibration. If placed in water it dissolves, so do not cleanse it this way. It brings incomparable peace and is said to facilitate contact with angels. If you have chosen selenite, you may have deep within you a concern for your past lives and evolutionary path, and instinctively wish to be on the right track. This stone enables you to check, intuitively, whether you are fulfilling the tasks necessary in this lifetime.

BLACK OBSIDIAN

This is an extremely powerful stone. There is no messing around with black obsidian; it will haul the truth up out of the depths so that it can be confronted and transmuted. Use this stone with care and be sure it is right for you. If you have chosen black obsidian, you may feel you need to face certain aspects of yourself and/or certain memories before you can progress spiritually.

Black obsidian will help you transform, changing negative to positive. It will also confer strength and protection. Placed on the Solar Plexus Chakra, this stone brings subtle energies into the body and has a grounding effect. Scrying with obsidian may result in prophecy, but this should be used with care.

Your choice of obsidian shows COURAGE, and a WISH to MOVE forward.

....
....
....
....
....
....
....
....
....
....
....
....
....
....
....

SODALITE

Sodalite induces deep meditative states, fostering the search for truth and idealistic values. If you have chosen sodalite, you seek the conviction to stand up for your beliefs, coming from a position not of believing but knowing. Sodalite sweeps away dogmatism and blinkered thinking, enabling both intuitive understanding and objectivity.

Placed on the Third Eye Chakra, it enables you to have a true understanding of your situation in life. Sodalite increases self-esteem and self-reliance, so that you can practise what you preach. It also helps you to accept the things about yourself that are shadowy and unpleasant, without judgement or guilt.

This stone indicates that you want to be FREE of preconception and indoctrination, to find your own CONNECTION with the DIVINE.

....
....
....
....
....
....
....
....

....
....
....
....
....
....
....
....
....

This is a very positive stone and can also help to achieve SPIRITUAL EXPERIENCES through SEX and to perceive its SACREDNESS.

....
....
....
....
....
....
....
....
....
....
....
....
....
....
....
....
....

RHODOCHROSITE

This warm pink or orange stone encourages you to open your Heart Chakra to trust and to love. If you have chosen rhodochrosite, you may want to access inspiration from your subconscious in order to be artistically and creatively inspired. You may have been hurt or abused, and you realize that only by getting to the root of this and releasing it can you switch on to the Universal love that is all around. You can facilitate this by placing rhodochrosite on the Solar Plexus or Base Chakras while relaxing.

Rhodochrosite helps you to accept all your feelings as natural. Choice of this stone may indicate that your emotions have been a barrier to meditation, or that you have an ardent desire to be an active, loving and spiritual participant in the world.

MEDITATION
RITUALS

The following pages contain rituals, meditations
and visualizations for you to practise.

Working with your Meditation Crystal can be a valuable
method of self-reflection, and it can help you to explore
situations and feelings more deeply.

Use the journal spaces to record your experiences
as you practise these rituals and connect with your
Meditation Crystal.

SCRYING MEDITATION

Scrying is actually crystal gazing, although you can scry using almost anything with a reflective surface, even a bowl of water. As you look deeply into your speculum (the object you are using for scrying), you are tuning into images in your subconscious that may be helpful, revealing or even prophetic. Your own Meditation Crystal is the perfect vehicle for you to look within and beyond.

You will need a candle; frankincense or sandalwood oil.

1. Scrying is a solemn matter and it is better to do it when you feel strong and upbeat; if you are depressed, you may call negative images your way or interpret things badly. Prepare for scrying by first taking a bath or shower, possibly using lavender soap for spiritual cleansing. Affirm that you are clear, calm and protected – it is a good idea to visualize a protective circle of light around you.

2. It is best to scry in a darkened room. Lighting a candle can help to set the scene, and you may prefer to scry with the candle flame reflecting in the surface of your crystal. Moonlight is even better. In an oil burner, heat oil with an uplifting fragrance such as frankincense or sandalwood.

3. Sit in a relaxed way with your crystal in your lap or on a flat surface in front of you – the larger your crystal is, the easier you will find this, and the clichéd crystal ball is best of all. However, it is possible to scry with a small, rough stone. If your stone is very small, then place it beside a bowl of water and use the water as your speculum.

4. If you have a question, ask it clearly in your mind before you start. Allow yourself to become dreamy, almost as if you are about to go to sleep, but without feeling tired.

5. Look deeply into your speculum, as if you were looking into another world. Soon you should see images – some people experience these as if they were literally "seeing" them, others see with the "mind's eye". You may not see anything, but you may find that you hear, feel, taste or even smell things. Your crystal can put you in touch with messages in many different ways. Even if something does not appear to make sense, it may become apparent later.

Sometimes things you see can be alarming, but a skull, for instance, can mean ancestral wisdom, so you should always look for a positive interpretation.

6. When you have finished scrying, imagine a clear, sparkling stream running through your crystal, cleansing it of any impurities. Wrap it up in black velvet and put it away safely. Make sure you have come back fully to everyday awareness by patting your body and affirming that your protective circle has vanished. Stamp your feet to reconnect with the earth and take a drink of water or tea. If you practise scrying regularly, your talents will develop.

Did you ask any questions before you began? If so, what were they, and do you feel you uncovered the answers? Journal about everything you saw, even if you don't understand it at the moment. How did you feel as you explored this other world? How did it look, feel, smell, taste?

....
....
....
....
....
....
....
....
....
....
....
....
....
....
....
....

REACHING OUT TO YOUR CRYSTAL ANGEL VISUALIZATION

This visualization will help you make contact with the spirit of love and wisdom to which your crystal is a portal. It is intended to be a deeper and more intimate encounter than you made when choosing your crystal. Here, your crystal spirit is not only companion and guardian but teacher.

Before you begin, think about what it will be like to meet your crystal spirit. Are you excited? Nervous? Scared? Calm? Do you have any questions for them? What would you like to say to them?

....
....
....
....
....
....
....
....

1. Prepare for this exercise in the same way as for scrying, by bathing and heating oil in an oil burner, as this helps to get you in the right frame of mind. Settle yourself where you can relax totally. Place your crystal in front of you where you can see it as you enter your inner world. You may prefer to make a voice recording of the following instructions before starting the ritual.

2. Imagine that it is the cool of evening and the bright crescent of the new moon hangs in a lilac sky. You find yourself at the foot of a beautiful mountain, made solely of the substance of your crystal. You touch the sides to find that they are smooth and invite caress. Now notice a staircase cut into the side of the mountain. You begin to ascend the steps slowly and smoothly.

3. Higher and higher you climb, and, as you do so, the shadowy landscape stretches around you and beneath you. Up and up you go, where the air is pure and clear, until you come to a platform where the staircase ends. There is a door with a silver handle leading into the mountain. Gently turn the handle and walk in.

4. You find yourself in a place of breathtaking beauty. The walls within the crystal mountain sparkle and shimmer. The chamber extends far into the distance and the ceiling is high. A subtle light illuminates everything. There is a sound of soft music and a scent of incense. You feel full of wonder.

5. At the far end of the chamber the light seems to be growing. You watch as it increases in intensity and you realize that a being of great power and beauty is coming toward you. This is the spirit of your crystal. They will appear to you in the way that is best to communicate with you.

6. Greet your crystal spirit in any way that seems appropriate. Ask them any questions that you have and listen carefully to the answers. Your crystal spirit may say things to you unbidden, and you should listen to these as well. Your crystal spirit will have a gift for you; this may be something abstract, like love or courage, or something real and symbolic, such as a book. Whatever this is, treasure it and give thanks. Pledge also a gift of your own that seems appropriate, such as a loving act. Remain with your spirit as long as feels right.

7. When you are ready, take leave respectfully, make your way to the door and down the mountainside. When you reach the bottom, come back to everyday awareness. Pat yourself to make sure that you are back in the here and now, and have a drink of water or tea.

8. Each time you travel to meet your crystal spirit, you will be forging a stronger connection with the spirit of your crystal. This will help to foster peace, wisdom and a deep knowledge.

How did you feel when you saw your crystal spirit? What did they say to you? What gift did the spirit give you, and what did you promise in return? Record all your experiences in as much detail as you can.

....
....
....
....
....
....
....
....
....
....
....
....
....
....
....
....
....
....
....
....
....
....
....
....
....
....

YOUR
LOVE
CRYSTAL

Love is top of the list of "wants" for most of us. We all need to be needed, we all want to feel part of something warm and close. However, there are many barriers to love. These may come from early conditioning and experiences or simply from expectations that are too high, shyness or fear.

In our times, we enjoy a great deal of freedom when it comes to choosing a partner, and we are in a position to decide very firmly what will and will not do. But with freedom comes responsibility, and with choice may come disappointment, as it may be very difficult for reality to match up to the fantasy we have fixed upon.

Your Love Crystal will help you to deal with important issues and dissolve the barriers that come between you and the love and closeness you desire. In addition, it can help you overcome the two greatest and simplest obstacles of all. The first of these concerns is loving yourself. Unless you love yourself, unless you have self-esteem, self-worth, you will find it very hard to attract someone who truly loves and respects you, because you are just not giving out the right "vibes". The second concerns the ability to love. Can you open your heart? Can you feel true empathy and give of yourself? In order to have a lover, you need to be a lover. In the game of love the stakes can be high – your Love Crystal will weight the dice in your favour and so help you find the love and fulfilment you need.

CHOOSING YOUR LOVE CRYSTAL

Many crystals are connected to love in some form or fashion, but some are especially appropriate. The following have been selected for their links to love. Some – especially diamond – may be quite expensive, but if you cannot purchase all of the stones in raw or tumble-stone form, maybe you could borrow some in jewellery from a friend, buying for yourself the one that turns out to be "yours". Use the journal spaces to record your experiences as you discover your Love Crystal.

YOU WILL NEED

Choose from:
rose quartz, amber, lapis lazuli, ruby, emerald, diamond, sapphire, angelite, amethyst, brown agate, golden calcite and hematite.

Rose- or pink-coloured cloths and candles; rose petals.

Before you start, think about what love means to you at the moment, and what you would like your Love Crystal to help you achieve.

....

....

....

....

....

....

....

....

....

....

....

....

THE MEDITATION METHOD

This method is more general than the Rose Visualization method on the next page, and may serve if you are older and experienced, and have memories that are less than happy.

Start by laying out the crystals before you on a rose- or pink-coloured cloth and burn a candle of the same colour | Sprinkle pink or red rose petals around the crystals | Sit in front of the crystals feeling relaxed and harmonious | If you have some memories you prefer not to recall, allow your mind to focus on something uplifting, such as a beautiful tree or flower; there is no need to think about any specific human love | Relax until you are able to think positively and are ready to be kind to yourself | Allow a sensation of warmth and openness to begin in your chest | Slowly feel it expanding, wider and wider, taking in the whole world in joy and love | Be aware of all the wonderful things that surround you | When you are ready, let your attention come back to the crystals | Which one best fits this glow in your heart?

At the end of this ritual it is very important that you close down your subtle senses, so imagine your heart closing up, like the petals of a wonderful flower, folding back into a tight bud. Eat and drink something and pat your body, to affirm that you are "back". This ritual involves you opening yourself up, so it is important not to leave yourself vulnerable. You should feel encouraged and filled with faith in your crystal.

What did you find yourself thinking about and focusing on at the start of the exercise? Which crystal did you choose, and what about it made you reach for it? What kind of energy does your newly chosen Love Crystal seem to have?

....

....

....

....

....

....

....

....

....

....

THE ROSE VISUALIZATION METHOD

If you have been able to obtain all of the crystals, lay them out before you on a rose- or pink-coloured cloth and burn a candle of the same colour | Sprinkle pink or red rose petals around the crystals | Clear quartz may be substituted for diamond (but if diamond turns out to be your choice, you will need to obtain the real thing) | If you do not have the crystals, you may use substitutes, such as names written on coloured paper or glass beads of the correct colour: because love is so strong an emotion, it may be possible to make your choice with no actual crystals present. The choice may just arrive in your mind as you do the visualization.

Close your eyes and relax, allowing your mind to go into a dreamy state | Now think of a time when you felt really, truly loved and treasured, or simply a time when you felt confident of your lovability | Or think of a time when you felt love, very strongly and deeply, for another person | Which crystal fits that feeling? Your eyes may open and alight on a particular crystal, or you may just "know" deep inside.

Which crystal did you choose, and what about it seemed to draw you toward it? What was the feeling you were focusing on before you chose the crystal?

....
....
....
....
....
....
....
....
....
....

The drawback with this method may be that it harks back to a former ruptured relationship, to a ring you had or some other memento. If so, try the meditation method on page 109.

If this method brought up any difficult feelings for you, you can journal about them here.

....
....
....
....
....
....
....
....
....
....

INTERPRETING YOUR LOVE CRYSTAL

This section will help you interpret your Love Crystal. Pay attention to the different elements of each crystal, and consider how this relates to your own experiences and feelings about love. Your crystal may reveal things to you about your desires and needs that you haven't really recognized before. Use the spaces to journal about what you learn.

ROSE QUARTZ

One of the most truly loving crystals of all, rose quartz brings peace, acceptance, healing and affection. If you have chosen rose quartz, your heart may need to be soothed after a broken romance or you need to be able to trust once more. This stone will help you forgive yourself and release old patterns that are keeping you from love – it enables repressed emotions to be released.

Of course, it is also possible that you have chosen this stone because you have a great deal of love within you to give to others. So great are its loving powers that you may find wearing it draws more attention your way than you can handle.

Rose quartz will help you to EMPATHIZE and to RECEIVE UNDERSTANDING.

....
....
....
....
....
....
....
....
....

AMBER

Not really a stone but tree-resin, amber brings with it the vibrant life force of the earth. If you have chosen amber you may need to have your faith in love restored in order to be enthusiastic about relationships and to be able to see the best in others. Amber empowers you to make the best of yourself and to exude warmth and responsiveness; it has been used through the ages to enhance beauty and sex appeal and to dispel loneliness.

It increases fertility and sexual prowess. This gem also helps to increase sensual pleasure and abandonment by its link with the powers of the natural world. Worn near the heart, it has the power to attract a mate.

Amber brings HAPPINESS at all levels but especially in the REALM of RELATIONSHIPS.

....
....
....
....
....
....
....
....
....
....
....
....
....
....
....
....
....

AMETHYST

This very spiritual and tranquil stone brings contact with higher realms yet also helps with common sense. If you have chosen amethyst you may wish to connect with another at a very deep level, and you may desire to be uplifted and inspired. It is possible you feel that past relationships have been too focused on the material or you may simply be most at home on the spiritual plane, which does not mean you lack sensuality but that you see the body as a vehicle for spirit.

It calms self-destructive passions and addictive behaviour patterns. Amethyst can show you another reality without encouraging self-deception. It is a stone of unconditional love and may awaken psychic senses, so that you "know" how others feel.

Traditionally, amethyst was EXCHANGED by LOVERS to signify COMMITMENT.

....
....
....
....
....
....
....
....

....
....
....
....
....
....
....
....

....
....
....
....
....
....
....
....
....
....
....
....

BROWN AGATE

Agate has a stabilizing and strengthening effect, encouraging inner balance. If you have chosen agate as your Love Crystal you may need to be honest with yourself about your feelings. Pent-up negative emotions such as spite and jealousy can keep you from attracting love, since others may be aware of this at an instinctive level.

Agate heals, helps you to feel safe and relaxes you to accept yourself as you are and so receive love. Of course, you may also have chosen agate because you are level-headed and sensible, and wish to enhance this. Agate has long been used in love-spells, to draw on the bounty of the Earth.

This stone helps you to find PRACTICAL solutions in matters to do with love, relationships and generally ATTRACTING a MATE.

LAPIS LAZULI

This lovely blue stone is very powerful, having ancient associations with royalty and with the goddess Isis. It can help you express yourself with confidence and dignity. If you have chosen lapis lazuli you may have had experiences in the past that made you feel demeaned, and you now wish to enhance your self-worth. It may also mean that your priority in relationships is a sense of self-respect, pride and fulfilment.

Lapis lazuli ensures dignity, equality and true communication. It also helps the psychic powers, enabling you to tune in to the needs and feelings of others, if you so wish. It has long been considered a fidelity charm and lovers may wear it to strengthen the bonds between them.

In general, this stone brings PEACE and a LOVE that UNITES the physical, mental, emotional and spiritual levels.

....
....
....
....
....
....
....
....
....
....
....
....
....
....
....
....
....

RUBY

Polished ruby is expensive but it is possible to get uncut stones. This rich red stone comes replete with energy and passion. If you have chosen ruby it is likely that you want to liven up your social life and have lots of sex. You may also desire a passionate love affair that involves you deeply, with lots of physical expression and extravagant romance.

However, if you tend to be a bit hyperactive, ruby can have a calming effect on you, helping you to focus on what you feel and do. Ruby jewellery has long been worn to drive out sadness and to attract riches of all descriptions.

Ruby confers a LUST for LIFE, and gives you COURAGE when meeting new people or going out on dates.

....
....
....
....
....
....
....
....
....
....
....
....
....
....
....
....
....
....

SAPPHIRE

Pure blue sapphire is a spiritual stone that reveals the truth and brings clarity. You may have chosen sapphire if you have been confused about a relationship and about what you want from love, or your ability to be lovable and loving (or indeed whether you truly want love at all). You may also be drawn to sapphire if you want honesty and open communication in a relationship above all things and to share similar ideals.

Sapphire brings peace and fidelity, a "meeting of true minds". It was once used to ensure chastity, but this may also be taken to mean a restriction of sexual activity to a committed partner.

This stone GUARDS love from any THREAT, internal or external, and oils the wheels socially, so that romantic CONTACTS can be made.

....
....
....
....
....
....
....
....

....
....
....
....
....
....
....
....
....

DIAMOND

Although this stone is now a favourite for engagement rings, its association with love is fairly recent. The diamond's brilliance is also of fairly recent origin, following the discovery that pressure on the correct point allows the stone to be cut into many facets. Diamonds are wonderful for enhancing self-confidence with the opposite sex, and if you need a boost in this, you may well be drawn to diamond. However, this scintillating stone is a natural choice if you are an extravert and relish being the centre of attention.

Diamond increases energy at all levels and cuts through any deception or murkiness, so you cannot kid yourself or be content with second best. It brings a clear expression of needs and feelings and gives you the courage to tackle difficult issues. This stone has long been linked with abundance.

Diamonds HEAL quarrels and ensure FIDELITY between LOVERS.

....
....
....
....
....
....
....
....
....
....
....
....
....
....
....
....

EMERALD

The brilliant green of emerald is representative of our planet Earth and all her riches. For eons, wearing an emerald close to your heart has been used as a way of attracting a lover. If you have chosen emerald, you may have been through a bad time and need the strength to overcome this, but also to count the good things you do have, to amplify them and enjoy them to the full.

Emerald's loving influence facilitates setting up home with your lover. This stone helps understanding and wisdom, but it also brings material benefits so that the marriage bed may be filled with delights and the table laden with good food.

Emerald ensures that lovers will also be friends, and brings the PATIENCE to RESOLVE issues and establish SECURITY.

....
....
....
....
....
....
....
....
....
....
....

ANGELITE

This blue-white stone is very much in keeping with the New Age and its message of human brother- and sisterhood. If you have chosen angelite your ideas and wishes with regard to relationships may be unconventional. You may like an "open" type of relationship where you are principally a friend to your lover, or have several relationships which you conduct in a broad-minded, honest and relaxed fashion. Maybe you do not particularly want demands or involvement, but prefer affection and friendliness with all. Or it may be that you seek a true spiritual bonding.

There is much compassion and peace with this stone. If you have had bad experiences of intimacy it will enable you to interact with warmth, remaining self-contained and yet totally honest with yourself and others about your motives and feelings.

It is a good stone to facilitate TELEPATHIC COMMUNICATION between LOVERS.

....
....
....
....
....

....
....
....
....
....
....
....
....
....
....

GOLDEN CALCITE

This cleansing, clearing stone amplifies energies. If this is your choice you may feel emotionally contaminated and that the loves you have had have been grounded in unhealthy patterns or cravings. Golden calcite helps you to use your emotional intelligence and to fall in love with your head as well as your heart. It will harmonize with you if you prefer to have your head rule your heart, enabling both sides to have their say.

Calcite prevents you from getting carried away, at the same time magnifying positive energy, keeping you quick-witted and resourceful. It enables you to trust your judgement in love matters. Calcite encourages fair and mature relationships, but it is also good for flirting and fun.

It brings lightness, BRIGHTNESS and OPPORTUNITIES for creating a loving future, filled with creative POTENTIAL.

....
....
....
....
....
....
....
....
....
....
....
....
....
....
....

HEMATITE

This silvery-black stone is a powerful grounder and protector. If you have chosen it you may want to come down to earth after a relationship that involved illusion or deception – including self-deception – or you may want to be emotionally or physically protected. It helps overcome sexual cravings and it strengthens willpower and courage. It is a good friend if

involved in the legalities of divorce, but on a positive note it helps you to make the most of your assets and to enhance your sex appeal in a very earthy way.

Because it draws attention and consciousness very much into the physical, it can aid orgasm. When bonding with a lover it enables you to focus on each other's creature comforts, strengthening the sensual bonds that are between you.

Hematite PROTECTS any commitment made from OUTSIDE interference and brings COMFORT and closeness.

....
....
....
....
....
....
....
....
....
....
....
....
....
....
....
....

LOVE
RITUALS

The following pages contain rituals, meditations and visualizations for you to practise.

Working with your Love Crystal can help you feel more connected with your emotions and gain clarity about what it is you truly desire. It can also help you to focus some of your loving energy on yourself.

Use the journal spaces to record your experiences as you carry out these rituals.

LOVING YOURSELF EXERCISE

To attract the love of another person, the first requirement is to love yourself; unless you truly believe you are lovable it is hard to radiate that magnetic confidence. Your crystal can help you attain that inner glow.

1. Do this exercise in the bath. Choose bath salts or oils to coordinate with the colour of your crystal and place as many candles as you like of the same colour in the bathroom. Make sure the bathroom is warm and that you have a snuggly towel and soothing lotion for after-bath pampering. Place your Love Crystal where you can see it while you are in the bath, and surround it with candles. If possible have more than one crystal. However, to be on the safe side do not place your crystal in the bath, for some oils can have a detrimental effect on some crystals.

2. Rub the bathwater gently and sensually all over your body, saying "Feet, I love you. Legs, I love you", continuing until you have covered your whole body with love. Imagine all the good things that part of your body does. Visualize yourself glowing with the power of your crystal. Concentrate on your positive attributes, feel warm, imagine compliments, embraces, caresses and pampering.

3. When you are ready, leave your bath, towel dry, rub in lotion (repeating self-loving affirmations) and give yourself a treat.

You can repeat this exercise as often as you like.

How did it feel to lavish such care and attention on yourself? Were there times when you found it challenging? Write about it here.

....
....
....
....
....
....
....
....
....

ATTRACTING LOVE RITUAL

The essence of your crystal can help you draw towards yourself the love that you want.

You will need a narrow glass; larger glass bowl or jug; orange or gold candle; vodka or brandy.

1. Find the narrowest glass you have, such as a liqueur glass or jam jar, and place your crystal at the bottom of this. Place the narrow glass in a much larger bowl, glass or jug and pour still spring water into the larger vessel so that it comes close to the top of the smaller glass without overflowing into it. (It is better to do this than to place the crystal directly into water as some crystals are friable or toxic.)

2. Place the bowl on the windowsill on a sunny day so that it absorbs sunlight for most of the day. If you are able to time this exercise for the full moon, follow this by placing it in moonlight for a similar span of time. If the weather is cloudy and you wish to do this without delay, wait until the evening and light a big, thick orange or gold candle and leave the crystal in the candlelight for as long as you can. Affirm that the energies of your crystal are being magnified and radiating out into the water in the surrounding bowl.

3. Now place the charged gem-water in a sterilized bottle. Before going out on a date or hoping to meet a lover, sip a little of the elixir, feel it entering your body with warmth and power and affirm that you radiate magnetism and the glow of your crystal. Imagine the radiance surrounding you, drawing love to you. You may dab the elixir over your body, behind your ears or on more intimate parts.

How do you feel when you use the elixir? Desirable? Adored? Sensual?

....

....

....

....

....

....

....

....

OPEN YOUR HEART VISUALIZATION

If you have been hurt or disillusioned, you may close your heart; despite the fact that you consciously want to draw love toward you, unconsciously you may be giving off signals that say "keep out".

1. Before this visualization, be honest and ask yourself if you are creating a blockage. Do you truly want to attract a lover? Maybe you just want to have a little more trust, enjoyment and fun in life. Try to sort out what you really want. Lie down where you will not be disturbed and place your crystal on your heart. Breathe steadily and allow yourself to feel relaxed and peaceful.

2. Now feel a glow starting in your chest, where your crystal is. Regardless of the colour of your crystal, imagine this glow as a wonderful shimmering green. Feel this glow extending, going outwards into the world. Feel love for all things – all the plants and animals that are on the Earth, all the people that inhabit it. Think of beautiful things – majestic trees, panoramic views, blossom, sunshine, sun-kissed waves and a feeling of joy pervading all.

3. When you are ready to come back to everyday awareness, ground yourself by closing down your subtle senses; imagine your heart closing up like the petals of a flower. Eat and drink something and pat your body, to affirm that you are "back".

Light a joss stick as an offering to whatever cosmic power you believe in, giving thanks for the experience.

If you acknowledged that you were creating a blockage, what was it? Do you feel this ritual has helped to remove it?

....
....
....
....
....
....
....
....
....
....
....
....
....
....

YOUR MONEY CRYSTAL

Depending on your personality and circumstances, you will have your own specific requirements with regard to money. Some people are very good at managing or acquiring money; others are not.

Circumstances vary from person to person. You may need money urgently for some particular project or purpose, or you may have received a legacy and need to spend and invest wisely. Psychological issues around money may be more important for you; for instance, do you have a "poverty consciousness", where you behave as if you are poor, even when you are comfortably off? Or does money just run through your fingers? Maybe you are a retail junkie or find it hard to budget. Maybe you are drawn to gambling, or you simply keep losing your purse. Whatever the issues and the situation, your choice of Money Crystal can help you become balanced and prosperous.

It is best to have a sample of each of the crystals as tumble-stones, but if this is not possible, then use pictures of the particular crystals. However, you may find the final method of selection difficult to perform if you only use paper representations.

CHOOSING YOUR MONEY CRYSTAL

Before selecting your crystal, it is important to relax and to reflect on your needs and situation in life. This allows you to focus your consciousness on the choice, although sometimes the crystal chosen has a message of its own that helps you to understand yourself better. This is part of the crystal gift. Use the journal spaces provided to record your experiences and feelings as you go through the process of choosing your Money Crystal.

YOU WILL NEED

Tumble-stones of the following crystals:
jade, tiger's eye, aventurine, bloodstone, calcite, chrysoprase, peridot, sapphire, green tourmaline, gold topaz, green quartz and spinel.

Green candle; gold candle; oil or joss sticks of patchouli; green cloth; organic brown rice; earthenware bowl.

Before you begin, take a moment to reflect on any money issues you hope to address with the help of your crystal.

....

....

....

....

....

....

....

....

....

....

....

....

THE CLOTH BAG METHOD

Follow the method on page 71 and think clearly about your finances and what you would most like help with.

THE CANDLE METHOD

Lay the tumble-stones or pictures out before you on a green cloth (green is traditionally associated with money) | Light a green candle behind the crystals and place your credit card, purse or wallet in front of them | Place any other article or document that is especially important to your finances there as well | Sit in front of your stones and close your eyes | Ask to be shown the stone that will be most helpful to you in your financial situation | When you are ready, open your eyes | You should now have a sense of which crystal to choose – probably the one on which your eyes alighted first, or your choice may be indicated by shadows thrown by the candle.

Finances can be a difficult subject for many of us. How did you feel as you began this process? Vulnerable? Cautious? Excited? Which crystal did you choose? How did you feel when you made a connection to that crystal?

....
....
....
....
....
....
....
....
....

THE RICE BOWL METHOD

You will need the actual tumble-stone versions of your crystals for this method and some organic brown rice in an earthenware bowl (because of its nourishing qualities, rice is traditionally linked to wealth).

Lay out your crystals before you on a green cloth with the green and gold candles | Light the candles and the patchouli incense/oil and sit, relaxed, in front of the crystals | Place your right hand (if right-handed) into the bowl of rice and indulge yourself with a fantasy of wealth | Now pick up the crystals in turn while you imagine this abundance.

Describe the fantasy you used for this process, and also how you felt as you touched each crystal. Which one enhanced your fantasy the best? Did the fantasy shift or change as you touched the different crystals?

....
....
....
....
....
....
....
....
....
....
....

You may have to do this exercise several times, eliminating crystals each time until you arrive at your final choice. You will then be left with your Money Crystal.

THE CRYSTAL CIRCLE METHOD

Try this if you feel you have a special money problem that you wish to overcome, such as gambling.

Do it on a green cloth or carpet if possible | Burn oil or a joss stick of patchouli and place your crystals or their substitutes in a wide circle on the cloth | Sit in the centre of the circle and think about your problem | Visualize yourself in the situation that you find difficult to control; for instance, when you are out shopping | In this situation you need a guardian at your elbow to restrain you with good advice | Imagine this gentle, wise and firm guardian is arising out of one of the crystals.

Which crystal is it?

....

....

....

THE VISUALIZATION METHOD

If you are able to visualize and have an emotional issue concerning money, this may be a good method for you.

Lay your crystals out as described in the Candle Method, without bothering with the documents and credit cards. Sit in front of the crystals or their representations and imagine yourself in the relevant challenging situation, such as speaking to your bank manager or negotiating a settlement with your ex.

Now, which of the crystals do you most want to hold in your hand?

....

....

INTERPRETING YOUR MONEY CRYSTAL

These pages will offer you some guidance on how to interpet your Money Crystal. Read the description and see if it resonates with you and your current understanding of your relationship with money. Journal about how you feel as you learn more about your chosen crystal.

JADE

This stone helps you to think positively about money, to value what you possess, and enables you to use it wisely. It stimulates your creativity with regard to money-making enterprises and has the ability to attract money. However, jade is a spiritual stone and will enable you to have a balanced attitude to your finances, realizing that the most important riches are not to be found in any bank account.

If you have chosen jade, then it may be that you need to stop worrying about money. This stone will help you to expel negative thoughts and to realize that management of money is essentially a simple matter. Wearing jade jewellery attracts money and helps you receive it gracefully.

Jade will help you to feel SELF-SUFFICIENT and INDEPENDENT, AWARE of the resources that you possess and able to utilize them.

....
....
....
....
....
....
....
....
....
....
....
....
....
....

TIGER'S EYE

This very protective stone was once worn as a protection against curses and all forms of danger. Tiger's eye is a fine stone to have if your finances are under any sort of threat, especially from theft or swindling. This stone is grounding and yet enlightening – it can enable you to see clearly "with the eye of the tiger". Because of this it can help you to recognize what your true needs are and to distinguish between your needs and those of other people.

If you have chosen tiger's eye then perhaps you feel your money is under threat. Or maybe you feel vulnerable because you have little trust in your ability to make money. Hold tiger's eye in sunlight and look within it to open your mind to inspiration.

Tiger's eye will give you FAITH in your talents and the STRENGTH to face and OVERCOME your weaknesses.

....

....

....

....

....

....

....

....

....

....

....

....

....

....

....

....

....

....

AVENTURINE

Aventurine attracts prosperity – it helps to turn situations that are apparently disadvantageous into opportunities for gain. It can help you to spot profitable alternatives such as niches in the market if you are in business, or companies that are about to "take off" if you are investing. Aventurine is the gambler's stone, bringing good luck but also fostering that state of calm that preserves a "poker face". It brings the peaceful poise that encourages intuition.

If you have chosen aventurine then maybe you need a little more courage, more "devil-may-care" in your attitude to money, not in order to be foolish, but gambling what you can well afford to lose in order to attract opportunity. Perhaps you have been too uptight about money or maybe you just need a boost of faith in yourself.

SPECULATE to ACCUMULATE. Carry aventurine whenever you take a CHANCE.

....

....

....

....
....
....
....
....
....
....
....
....
....
....
....
....

they deserve it or can be relied on.
A bloodstone kept in a till or cash register
is said to draw more money to it.

With the support of this stone a difficult
SITUATION can be TRANSFORMED
gradually and with hard work into one of
stability and secure PROSPERITY.

....
....
....
....
....
....
....
....
....
....
....
....
....
....

BLOODSTONE

This stone of strength can help you to
adjust to challenging circumstances. If
you have chosen bloodstone then you
may need to stop worrying about your
financial future and concentrate on the
here and now, since that is all you can
have control over.

If your money situation is satisfactory,
bloodstone protects your interests but
also enables you to judge whom to trust
and whom to avoid.

If you are considering helping someone
financially by lending or investing,
bloodstone will help you decide whether

GREEN CALCITE

Green calcite will help you to let go of old
mental patterns concerning money, such
as "poverty consciousness", beliefs such as
"I never win anything" or feelings of not
deserving to be rich. It can help you to
grow conceptually, so you can clearly

picture wealth, which is the first step toward gaining it.

If you have chosen calcite then perhaps you need to move away from your outworn beliefs about money and start picturing yourself as rich. Do not always buy the cheapest – send your subconscious messages of abundance by having the best once in a while. Calcite may double the effectiveness of an enterprise if placed in a significant spot, such as with contracts.

Calcite is especially good at DRAWING money into the HOME, so it should have pride of place in the "MONEY CORNER" or on the hearth next to a green candle.

....
....
....
....
....
....
....
....
....
....
....
....
....
....
....
....

CHRYSOPRASE

This stone helps you to feel part of a beautiful, inter-connected Universe. It promotes good faith in business interests and encourages a calm state of mind that brings openness to opportunity. It helps you to rise above compulsive and impulsive spending and to direct efforts and finances in positive directions.

If you have chosen chrysoprase you may need to leave behind an extravagance that brings you no enduring pleasure. It can stop you being greedy for that next retail "fix" and helps you to use money in accordance with your ideals. It will help you to see where you went wrong in the past and help you correct mistakes. Carry chrysoprase with you to attract money, especially if your income depends on "the gift of the gab".

Chrysoprase brings a sense of relaxation and TRUST in LIFE that invites LUCK.

....
....
....
....
....
....
....

....

....

....

....

....

....

....

....

....

....

....

....

....

....

....

PERIDOT

If you have bad habits with regard to money, peridot can help you leave these behind. If you tend to be miserly, this stone can help you see that this is counterproductive, and to set up a healthy flow of financial energy in your life. It can also banish envy, both your own and others, toward you, and protect you from jealous attack.

If you have chosen peridot then you may need to face certain attitudes that you have toward money and to recognize that these may not be healthy. This stone will stop you blaming others and help you to take full responsibility for your attitudes and actions. If you have business cards, it is a good idea to store them under a piece of peridot to infuse them with luck.

Peridot will help you form a clear IDEA of what CHANGES are NECESSARY and to bring them about.

SAPPHIRE

This stone attracts gifts in the form of wealth and possessions as well as more abstract gifts in the form of advice and information. It helps you to focus on the matter in hand and to feel cheerful and upbeat, believing that life is joyful.

If you have chosen sapphire it may be that you need a generous handout to help you out of a hole. Or perhaps you need an influx of energy, creativity and positive thought, which will attract money. Either way, the stone will help in attracting these things but also in maintaining serenity. It repels fraud and so is an effective stone to have if you are involved in any litigation involving money – as long as you are in the right.

Sapphire was considered especially MAGICAL by the ancients, with the power to STRENGTHEN any ENTERPRISE.

....
....
....
....
....
....
....
....
....
....
....
....
....
....

GREEN TOURMALINE

This calming and grounding stone enables you to appreciate the value of money, to be practical and to keep a balanced attitude.

It attracts gifts, but also encourages you to value what you already have, without continually hankering after extras.

If you have chosen green tourmaline you may need some patience and steadiness in your financial affairs. It may also indicate that you need to use your creativity to attract wealth. If you have been panicking over financial issues the gentle influence of this stone will enable you to get things in perspective. Place it in a money box to attract coins. Green tourmaline is especially good for giving you the CONFIDENCE and SERENITY to deal with your BOSS if he or she is something of a parent figure.

....
....
....
....
....
....
....
....
....
....
....
....
....
....
....
....

GOLD TOPAZ

A stimulating but soothing stone, topaz will help you to sort out short- and long-term financial goals and work toward them. If you have chosen topaz you may need to be put on track, or to make plans for your future. Or maybe you are financially well organized but need a little inspiration to make your money work harder for you.

It is a great stone to help in finding solutions to problems and will help you to throw light on details without losing the plot. In ancient times it was believed this stone could confer invisibility. Wear it to deflect the attention of anyone who is out to get your money, from thieves to traffic wardens.

Topaz makes you FEEL RICH, but also able to ENJOY all the things in life that MONEY CAN'T BUY.

....

....

....

....

....

....

....

....

....

....

....

....

....

....

GREEN QUARTZ

This stone will help you deal with waste, enabling you to husband your resources and get the most for least. If you have chosen green quartz you may feel that you are haemorrhaging money and need help to stem the flow. If money is not a problem, green quartz can stimulate your charitable instincts, enabling you to target your generosity wisely.

It stimulates the memory, enabling you to recall past mistakes so you do not repeat them, and to see how you created success, in order to build on it. Wear green quartz in order to attract the "easy life".

Green quartz has a wide range of INFLUENCE and will HEAL financial ILLS and imbalances of all descriptions.

....

....

....

....

....

....

....

....

....

....

....

....

....

....

....

....

....

a financial situation and that it is all too much, place spinel beside you on your desk for an influx of energy.

Traditionally, spinel attracts wealth, but will also give you the physical STRENGTH to EARN money and to FIGHT for what is yours – perhaps a legacy.

....

....

....

....

....

....

....

....

....

....

....

....

....

....

....

....

....

....

....

SPINEL

Spinel offers hope and encouragement even when things are at their most dire. If you have chosen spinel you may have been deluged by financial misfortune. This stone will enable you to laugh at your situation and turn the tide in your favour. On the other hand, if things are going well, spinel reminds you to give thanks where it is due and to retain humility.

It stimulates compassion so, if someone is being mean toward you, wear or display green spinel where they can see it. If you feel that you can't be bothered to sort out

MONEY RITUALS

The following pages contain rituals, meditations and visualizations for you to practise.

Working with your Money Crystal can help you develop a healthier approach to your finances, and improve your confidence in your ability to manage money.

Use the journal spaces to record your experiences of the rituals, and to note any changes you notice in your attitude toward and behaviour around money.

ATTRACTING ABUNDANCE VISUALIZATION

You can have an abundance of life's goodies – believe this is so and what you want will flow toward you. This is no great mystery, for if you change your consciousness and your beliefs, without realizing it you will begin to behave slightly differently. Gradually, you will start to attract wealth.

You will need a golden bowl, a cinnamon, patchouli or orange joss stick, some ears of wheat and a golden candle symbolizing the four traditional elements of water, air, earth and fire respectively; a large golden scarf to sit on. (If you cannot obtain ears of wheat, substitute almonds, pine nuts, acorns or rice in an earthenware dish.)

1. Lay out your scarf and place your bowl in the west, candle in the south, joss stick in the east and wheat/nuts in the north. If you live in the southern hemisphere, change the north/south placements. Light your candle and joss stick.

2. Face your candle, sitting comfortably with your crystal in your palm. Now imagine good news about jobs or payments flowing from the direction of your joss stick into your crystal, energy and opportunity from your candle, support from helpful people from your bowl and possessions and cash from your wheat/nuts. Feel the richness flow into you from the crystal.

3. Do this visualization for as long as is comfortable – a few minutes will do.

You can repeat it as often as you like. One of the good things about this exercise is that you will feel rich immediately!

How did you feel before the ritual? How about after? Do you have a sense of abundance flowing into your life? What was it like to visualize that richness and support?

....
....
....
....
....
....
....

HEALTHY ATTITUDE TO
MONEY MEDITATION

It is all too easy to fear poverty and this can paralyze wise investment of all kinds. The symbolism behind this little meditation will help you to relax and have faith in life's bounty.

1. Find a quiet place where you can unwind and won't be disturbed. Play music if you like. Doing this meditation in sunshine would be beneficial. If this is not possible, light a gold candle to set the mood while you settle. Place your crystal on your lap.

2. Imagine yourself sitting beside a golden stream, with your back propped up against a soft, mossy bank. Around you the grass is lush and green, and the sun is shining warm upon you. You can hear the singing of birds and the peaceful gurgle of the flowing water. In the air there is the scent of orange blossom, and in your hand you hold the smooth stem of a large goblet, made of your crystal.

3. Watch the rippling water as it glistens in the sunlight. It is clear and fresh, flowing ceaselessly onward, always moving, always plentiful. Look at it for a while, musing. Lean down and fill your goblet with the water – see how it sparkles! Empty and refill the goblet as many times as you wish; take a drink, if you like. Or you can simply relax, holding the goblet on your lap, savouring the peace. Do this for as long as you like.

4. When you are ready, come back to everyday awareness.

What thoughts occurred to you? How can you relate this ritual to your feelings around money?

....
....
....
....
....
....
....
....
....
....
....
....
....

WISE SPENDING RITUAL

Spending wisely means spending money for the right reasons (not just to cheer yourself up), making the right choices and keep to a reasonable budget. This means remaining in touch with your true wishes. Your crystal can keep you connected to these.

You will need your crystal in a bracelet in any form, either as a string of tumble-stones or polished and set in metal. It is also a good idea to have a small tumble-stone of your crystal to place in your purse or wallet.

You can do this ritual before shopping or at any time you feel the need.

1. Place your bracelet, tumble-stone and original crystal in front of you.

2. Gaze deeply at your crystal and close your eyes. Imagine the spirit of the crystal rising – it may take any form but brings with it a sense of wisdom, balance and practicality. Feel this spirit flowing all over you. Imagine the colour of your crystal emanating from it and surrounding you, forming a protective shield. This is your protection against unwise spending and is also a magnet for correct purchases. Hold this image for as long as feels comfortable and listen for any words or impressions that may come from the spirit.

3. When you are ready, thank the spirit and ask it to return to the crystal. Place the bracelet on your wrist, saying three times "Guard me from unwise spending, draw to me what I need". Place the tumble-stone in your purse or wallet – and go shopping!

When you return from shopping, write about it here. Did you feel like you were making better spending decisions?

....

....

....

....

....

....

....

....

....

....

....

YOUR
SUCCESS
CRYSTAL

Success means different things to different people, and
your own definition of "success" may well vary greatly
throughout your life, depending on times and
situations. Before you begin this process, take some
time to think about what success means to you, and
what kind of guidance and connection you hope a
Success Crystal will bring you.

In terms of your life as a whole, the meaning of success may change radically as you grow older. At some point in your life, success may be defined as "victory" – overcoming all odds, passing exams, getting a promotion – while at another point, success may be a much deeper matter of fulfilment, creativity and self-development.

While all crystals can help in self-development, your choice of the best crystal for you may change many times, and you may decide you need more than one at a time for different purposes. This is not so much about the crystals having very different properties individually (although they vary naturally), so much as facilitating different states in you.

To find true "success", it is helpful to be flexible and open-minded. You may find that your crystal stimulates ideas not only about how to attain your goals, but also how to formulate them.

CHOOSING YOUR SUCCESS CRYSTAL

Because your own definition of success will change depending on your circumstances, it is preferable to obtain all the crystals as tumble-stones or very small pieces, if possible. You may find that each one has its day. As you go through the process of selecting your crystal, use the spaces provided to journal about your experiences.

YOU WILL NEED

Choose from:
tiger's eye, dendritic (tree) agate, carnelian, holey stone, aventurine, citrine, hematite, green jasper, lepidolite, sodalite, sunstone, topaz.

Cinnamon sticks, green or gold cloths and candles, cinnamon oil or joss stick.

What does success mean to you at the moment? Have you felt differently about it at other points in your life?

....
....
....
....
....
....
....
....
....
....
....
....
....
....

THE MEDITATION METHOD

Spread the cinnamon sticks on a green or gold cloth, with the candles behind them; on the bed of cinnamon, lay out your selection of crystals, or their representation, on separate squares of paper | Burn a cinnamon joss stick or heat cinnamon oil, for good measure | Cinnamon is traditionally associated with prosperity and success | Now relax deeply with your eyes closed | Think of a time when you were really successful, when you felt as if you had the world at your feet, riding high, exultant | Fill yourself with this feeling | When you feel as "successful" as possible, hold your left hand (or your right, if you are left-handed) over the crystals | Keep your eyes closed, retaining the feeling and pass your hand slowly back and forth over the stones.

Note the sensations in your hand – does it feel hot or tingly, heavy or light? Is there a place where it feels most comfortable or to which it is drawn?

....

....

....

....

....

....

....

....

....

....

....

This is the place in the line-up where you will find your Success Crystal. If you are not quite sure which crystal is indicated, remove the definite "no"s and keep going until you have made the final choice.

THE VISUALIZATION METHOD ONE

The previous method assumes that, at some time, you have felt very successful, but this may not yet have happened to you in the way you want. However, are you able to visualize feeling really supreme?

If so, just imagine what it will be like when you are truly successful in the way you want to be and proceed as before.

Write a bit about the visualization you used and how it felt to imagine yourself feeling so successful. Which crystal did you choose? What made you pick that one?

....
....
....
....
....
....
....
....
....
....
....
....
....
....
....
....
....
....

THE VISUALIZATION METHOD TWO

This method is similar to the previous visualizations, but applies to some specific challenge at which you wish to succeed. If you are choosing your crystal for this you may need to choose again when the challenge is behind you, in order to find a crystal for more general success.

Imagine that you have succeeded at the challenge – for instance, passed an exam or won a race | Please do not imagine the specifics of the effort such as revising and writing reams or running like mad | Imagine instead the certificate, the trophy, the feeling of triumph and then proceed as in the first method as before.

Write about the challenge here, and how it felt to visualize yourself having succeeded at it. Which crystal spoke to you as you held this visualization in your mind?

....

....

....

....

....

....

....

....

....

....

....

....

....

....

INTERPRETING YOUR SUCCESS CRYSTAL

This section will teach you more about the properties of your Success Crystal. Does the description fit with your feelings about success? Is there anything there that surprises you? Use the spaces provided to journal about your newly chosen Success Crystal and what it means to you.

DENDRITIC AGATE

In general agate teaches self-reliance and self-value. It prevents you wasting energy envying and competing with others, and encourages you to understand your uniqueness. Dendritic agate has strong links with the earth and enables you to live in the present, valuing and experiencing each moment. If you have chosen dendritic agate, you may need to feel connected to your roots in order to discover your true path in life.

Dendritic agate brings stability and works slowly to help you find yourself. It creates peace and has very strong connections with the plant kingdom and nature spirits, so if you are looking for inspiration about your vocation, quiet time outdoors will clear your mind.

Dendritic agate will give you the strength to PERSEVERE, to see mistakes as learning EXPERIENCES and to PROGRESS.

....
....
....
....
....
....
....
....
....
....
....
....
....

AVENTURINE

This is a stone that will provide a bit of good, old-fashioned luck.

If you have chosen it then you may be

aware that the time has come for you to cast your fate to the wind and take a chance. Aventurine will enable you to be in the right state of mind to notice opportunities and simply to play with life to see what it brings. It may bring you a whole new set of circumstances and ideas or a new way of looking at the ones you've got. It may even bring you to the crock of gold. If you have any neuroses or nervous mannerisms, aventurine will enable you to understand what has caused them and to feel relaxed enough to leave them behind.

Aventurine will enable you to INSPIRE OTHERS and to be a LEADER, if that is what you want.

....
....
....
....
....
....
....
....
....
....
....
....
....
....
....

CARNELIAN

This very strong stone carries vitality and courage. If you have chosen carnelian then you are either feeling extremely ambitious and very determined to compete and succeed, or you are aware that you are going to be facing some tough challenges and that you need all the help you can get!

Carnelian will help you to draw on your deepest reserves and yet still have something left. It will also help you to target your efforts, laser-like, where they will have most effect. Carnelian makes your mind crystal clear, so you can formulate realistic goals and make your choices in life in a positive and empowered fashion.

Should you be feeling apathetic and despondent, this stone is just the TONIC you need to HELP you see that better things are POSSIBLE.

....
....
....
....
....
....
....
....

....
....
....
....
....
....
....
....
....
                                        ....
                                        ....
                                        ....
                                        ....

CITRINE

Citrine is a wonderful stone for making a new start. It will draw out your versatility and powers of invention, helping you to reinvent yourself and your life. It will toughen you against criticism and enable you to break the mould, to express your individuality and creativity. It is a stone of fun and bright ideas. If you have chosen it you may feel stuck in a rut, needing a shove in a new direction.

This stone sharpens your mind and enables you to tell other people what you think, how you feel and what you want. Because it is stabilizing to the mind it empowers you to take responsibility.

With citrine as your guide you will be prepared to EXPLORE and leave no stone unturned in your SEARCH for success and FULFILMENT.

HEMATITE

This is a stone for survivors. If it is your choice then you may feel that you have come through a very hard time. In fact, your whole life may have been shadowed and you could feel repressed. The time has come to end all that and to go back to basics, to count your assets, your health and to start building slowly and steadily. For the moment, success to you may be a matter of the practical and earthly and you are prepared to work hard and even be a little ruthless.

Hematite will show you what is driving you and can help you to HARMONIZE your SPIRIT with your BODY for more total fulfilment.

....
....
....
....
....
....
....
....
....
....
....
....
....
....
....
....
....

HOLEY STONE

A "holey stone" is not truly a crystal, but as the name says, a stone that has a naturally formed hole, caused by wind, wave, soil erosion, tiny creatures or any other means. Such stones can often be found on beaches and they can also be bought in New Age shops, along with crystals.

Because of the womb symbolism they are sacred to the Great Mother and have long been considered highly protective. If you have chosen holey stone then you may be realizing that your fulfilment lies in nurturing. Maybe you are trying to bring something to birth – if so this stone will support you. Perhaps you are wishing to intensify your links with the Earth and the Eternal Feminine offered by this stone.

Holey stone will help you ACCESS the riches of your UNCONSCIOUS mind, to free up creativity and ACT from the heart.

....
....
....
....
....
....
....
....
....
....
....
....
....
....

GREEN JASPER

This is a stone of balance and cooperation. It encourages discussion and helpfulness between the members of a community and helps you to understand where you have become lopsided, and helps correct this. If you have chosen green jasper, you may feel that your life is lacking in some respect and that you have lost contact with your soul.

This stone will help you find the missing parts of yourself, so that you feel whole. You may need to work less, play more, do active things if you have been office-bound, use your hands if you have been "in the head" and so on. Green jasper helps in self-realization and healthy self-love.

If you see SUCCESS in terms of being WELL ROUNDED, in loving and being loved by all, then green jasper is your friend.

....

....

....

....

....

....

....

....

....

....

....

....

....

....

....

....

LEPIDOLITE

Purple lepidolite is a spiritual stone and if you have chosen it then it is unlikely that you define your success in physical, practical terms, but in terms of your development as a human being and your enlightenment. Maybe you wish to help others but it is not the kudos that motivates you but the feeling of being a meaningful part of the cosmos.

This calming stone will stabilize your moods so you are better able to tune in to your life path. It will enable you to cut to the chase, dispensing with distractions and make important decisions. It will also help you succeed without the help of other people, whatever the undertaking.

Although it is SPIRITUAL, it will attract LUCK, and can bring REVELATIONS about your creative fulfilment in dreams.

It is an idealistic stone for those who measure success in terms of being true to themselves and doing good.

If you are planning charitable work, group sessions of some kind or teaching, sodalite will facilitate clear communication and an impeccable reputation. It enables you to inspire trust while also drawing the supportive presence of people of integrity.

Sodalite OPENS your MENTAL horizons and helps you UNDERSTAND many things, especially yourself.

SODALITE

This veined blue stone resembles lapis lazuli in appearance and brings gifts of intuition and spirituality. If you have chosen sodalite, your aspirations may be abstract. Perhaps you long for success in some form of higher study, or maybe you are learning a subtle skill such as healing or psychism. Sodalite keeps your logical mind in contact with your intuition so both prosper.

SUNSTONE

As the name suggests, this stone is for those who want to shine, to bask in the limelight. If you have chosen this stone then the chances are you want to see your name up in lights. Sunstone will remove inhibitions and free you from those who would hold you back, allowing your true self to shine through. It will also help you to stop making excuses and really go for what you want.

It strengthens you so that you can say "no" when this is necessary. Sunstone will give you inexhaustible physical energy when you are doing something creative or promoting yourself. However, it also reminds you to nurture yourself as the wonderful creature that you are.

Sunstone ENCOURAGES you to see the POSITIVE side and to turn disadvantage to ADVANTAGE.

....
....
....
....
....
....
....
....

....
....
....
....
....
....
....

TIGER'S EYE

This is a wonderful stone for energy, courage and luck. Its brown-yellow hues bring together the fire of the sun and the solidity of the Earth. If you have chosen tiger's eye then the chances are you are very ambitious but also aware that you must not overreach yourself.

This stone will help you keep your feet on the ground while you aim for the stars. Tiger's eye was traditionally carried as a talisman against ill-wishing and it will help you to be aware of anyone who is likely to do you harm and enable you to deal with them, bravely, firmly and sensibly. This stone will enable you to decide what you really need and what is just pie in the sky.

Tiger's eye helps you to NOTICE all RELEVANT data and to BRING the strands together.

It is also a very creative and artistic influence. If you have goals that are not quite formed in your mind topaz will help make them clear. It has the wonderful ability to enable you to see both the wood and the trees, and to see how they knit together.

The greatest gift of topaz is to REVEAL your abundant INNER RESOURCES, to delight in them and to use them.

....

....

....

....

....

....

....

....

....

....

....

....

....

....

....

....

....

....

TOPAZ

Vibrant topaz lights up the path of life and gives optimism and encouragement. If you have chosen topaz you are probably aware of the need for positive thinking. This stone will add power to your visualizations and affirmations and help you believe in yourself.

Topaz will also help you to value yourself and to realize just what you have to offer other people, so it supports confidence.

SUCCESS RITUALS

The following pages contain rituals, meditations and
visualizations for you to practise.

Working with your Success Crystal can help you feel more
optimistic and empowered, and it can also help your
recognize and appreciate areas in your life where you are
already successful.

Use the journal spaces to record your experiences as you
carry out these rituals.

ATTRACTING LUCK RITUAL

The best way to attract luck is a positive attitude and a happy outlook. This ritual will help you "feel" lucky. You can have an abundance of life's goodies – believe this is so and what you want will flow toward you, for if you change your consciousness and your beliefs, without realizing it you will begin to behave slightly differently. Gradually, you will attract wealth.

You will need eight tumble-stones of your Success Crystal; a horseshoe (or something to represent one; candle; orange oil.

1. Arrange seven of the tumble-stones in the horseshoe, then place the eighth in the "cup" of the horseshoe with the candle above it. Heat orange oil in an oil burner, for its optimistic "vibes".

2. Look at the candle flame and imagine all sorts of lucky things happening to you – meeting people, winning prizes, finding things. If big things seem too far-fetched, then just imagine small pieces of good fortune, such as finding what you want when you shop or getting a parking space. Let a big smile come over your face. Repeat "I am lucky, lucky, lucky!" as often as you wish.

3. Carry the eighth stone with you whenever you need a dose of luck. Leave the other seven crystals as ornaments if you wish, ready to recharge your luck crystal as often as you like. Cleanse all eight crystals if you start to think negatively and begin again.

What kind of lucky things did you imagine? How does the luck-charged crystal feel in your hand?

....
....
....
....
....
....
....
....
....
....
....
....
....
....

BOOST YOUR CONFIDENCE RITUAL

Confidence comes from being relaxed and having healthy self-esteem.
This exercise will remind you that you can achieve your goals.

**You will need a gold candle; a gold dish and any item of
jewellery with your special crystal on it; orange oil.**

1. Place the jewellery on the gold plate and put the candle in the centre, with the jewellery near the bottom of the candle. As you light it, say "I shine bright as this flame."

2. Touch your fingertips to the gold plate. Concentrate on your head. Feel a shining crown placed there, dazzlingly bright, so that all of your being is radiant. Feel it drawing you upward, so that your spine is straight. The radiance is going into your head, so your mind is bright and clear. Imagine yourself walking into a room, head held high, surrounded by this glow. Do not confront scary scenarios; now is the time to glow.

3. When you feel you have finished, wear your crystal and raise it to your head when you need to as a reminder that your "crown" is in place. If you need a boost, go off into a quiet place, hold your crystal on the top of your head and strongly imagine the crown glowing there.

**What is it like to wear
your imagined crown?
Do you feel bold?
Empowered? Confident?**

....
....
....
....
....
....
....
....
....
....
....
....
....
....
....
....
....